Cognac
a liquid History

ONAL INTERPROFESSIONNEL DU COGNAC
MISSION DE LA QUALITÉ
du
e du
N°
DELAMAIN

Cognac

a liquid History

SALVATORE CALABRESE

PHOTOGRAPHY BY
JASON LOWE

CASSELL ILLUSTRATED

To my wife, Sue

First published in the United Kingdom in 2001 by
Cassell & Co

This paperback edition printed in
2005 by Cassell Illustrated,
a division of the Octopus Publishing
Group Ltd,
2-4 Heron Quays,
London, E14 4JP

Photography by Jason Lowe

Managing Editor: Hilary Lumsden
Art Direction: Patrick Carpenter
Design: Grade Design Consultants
Editor: Jamie Ambrose

A CIP catalogue record for this book is available from the British Library.

ISBN-10 : 1844034755
ISBN-13 : 9781844034727

Printed and bound by Toppan in China

9 8 7 6 5 4 3 2

P2: THE RED WAX SEAL SIGNIFIES AUTHENTICITY OF VINTAGE COGNAC. PP4/5: A LEAD INTO THE CELLAR. OPPOSITE: A HYDROMETRE MEASURES THE VOLUME OF ALCOHOL IN A SPIRIT.

CONTENTS

1908
Hennessy
Divers

INTRODUCTION

THIS IS A PERSONAL STORY, AN EXPLORATION OF THE LAND, THE PEOPLE AND THE PRODUCTION OF THE FINEST DISTILLED SPIRIT IN THE WORLD: COGNAC. Called by many the 'noble' spirit, and (a more regal appellation) the 'king of brandies', cognac is imbued with a mystique that has fascinated me since I sipped my first Brandy Alexander back in the 1970s. I enjoyed the power of the cognac as it awakened my taste buds. That was the start of my love affair with this golden liquid that has captivated both men and women throughout the past three centuries.

PP8/9: INSIDE THE HENNESSY PARADIS ROWS OF ANCIENT CASKS HOLD AGEING COGNAC.

When I began my career in the bar business in Maori, on Italy's Amalfi coast, an elaborately shaped bottle of cognac was always on the bar shelf. In the 1970s and 1980s, if people wanted an after-dinner drink, they would usually ask for a cognac. I gradually learned to identify the different styles of individual cognac houses, also the difference between VS and XO. That, however, was the extent of my knowledge as a very young man.

Today, decades later, I have developed a deep and abiding passion for cognac and, in particular, rare vintage cognacs. During those preceding years, I set out on a journey to discover all I could about the production of cognac – which led me to discover both Vintage and Early Landed cognacs – and to research the history of the years they were bottled – you can read more about these in the last section of the book. What this extraordinary journey revealed to me was that the true spirit of cognac comes not just from the grape, but from the people of Charante, in the west of France, who plant, grow, pick, distil and produce the *eau-de-vie* that is cognac.

I first visited the region in the mid-1980s, after years of reading and experiencing the taste of different vintage cognacs. And until you visit this small country town – for Cognac is no more than a country town, with its bustling brasseries, numerous *coiffeuers* and *pâtisseries* – you do not truly understand exactly what the word 'cognac' on the label means. For cognac is a brandy made in a specific region of France. There are other French brandies made in other regions – for instance, Armagnac – but for me, there is only cognac.

On my most recent visit to the region, I flew into Bordeaux towards late summer of the year 2000, and as I drove from the airport I glimpsed a veritable verdant landscape neatly criss-crossed with vines. Their gnarled branches, leaves bright-green in the sunlight, were dripping with bunches of Ugni Blanc grapes, ripe and ready for picking.

The atmosphere was calm; it was just days before the harvest, and there was a tension in the air. Everybody was waiting for the grape-picking machinery to roar into life (few vineyards pick grapes by hand these days).

I turned the car off the road into a track among the vines, stopped and walked across the soil to have a closer look at the grapes. Each visit is an emotional experience for me because, for more than two decades, cognac has been an integral part of my life. The few grapes nestling in my hand were juicy, their skins ready to release the liquid held captive within. It looked as if the harvest would be plentiful. With a last look at the vines, I got back in the car to continue my journey to Cognac.

Occasionally, as I headed across country, I would see a small farmhouse. These belong to the growers, without whom the business would not exist. Most of them have a small private distillery on the property where they produce a small amount of *eau-de-vie* for their own consumption.

Driving through Jarnac, I saw the name 'Courvoisier' writ in large and bright capital letters above a riverside building, dominating the town. The River Charante was silent and still, as yet untouched by the later floods that would cause it to rise and gently lap at the front doors of the elegant properties built on the small side-road that runs parallel to the river.

Midway between Jarnac and Cognac – two towns still separated by an historic rivalry over many things (including religion) – I noticed the huge billboards advertising visits to cognac houses, so familiar to me from labels. Others were not so familiar, yet they probably produce fine cognac. Until you come to the region, you cannot comprehend just how many houses, large and small, there are in the area.

The town of Cognac came into view after a strip of light industrial buildings typical of many small country towns. The highway narrowed to a single lane, and within minutes I was in the town square with its statue of King François I in the centre. Ancient, narrow, cobbled streets lined with houses, their windows shuttered and closed to the casual visitor, tumbled down to the quayside of the River Charente. Here, three centuries ago, sailing ships unloaded their cargoes and took on board the rough wine produced by the region's growers for the return journey.

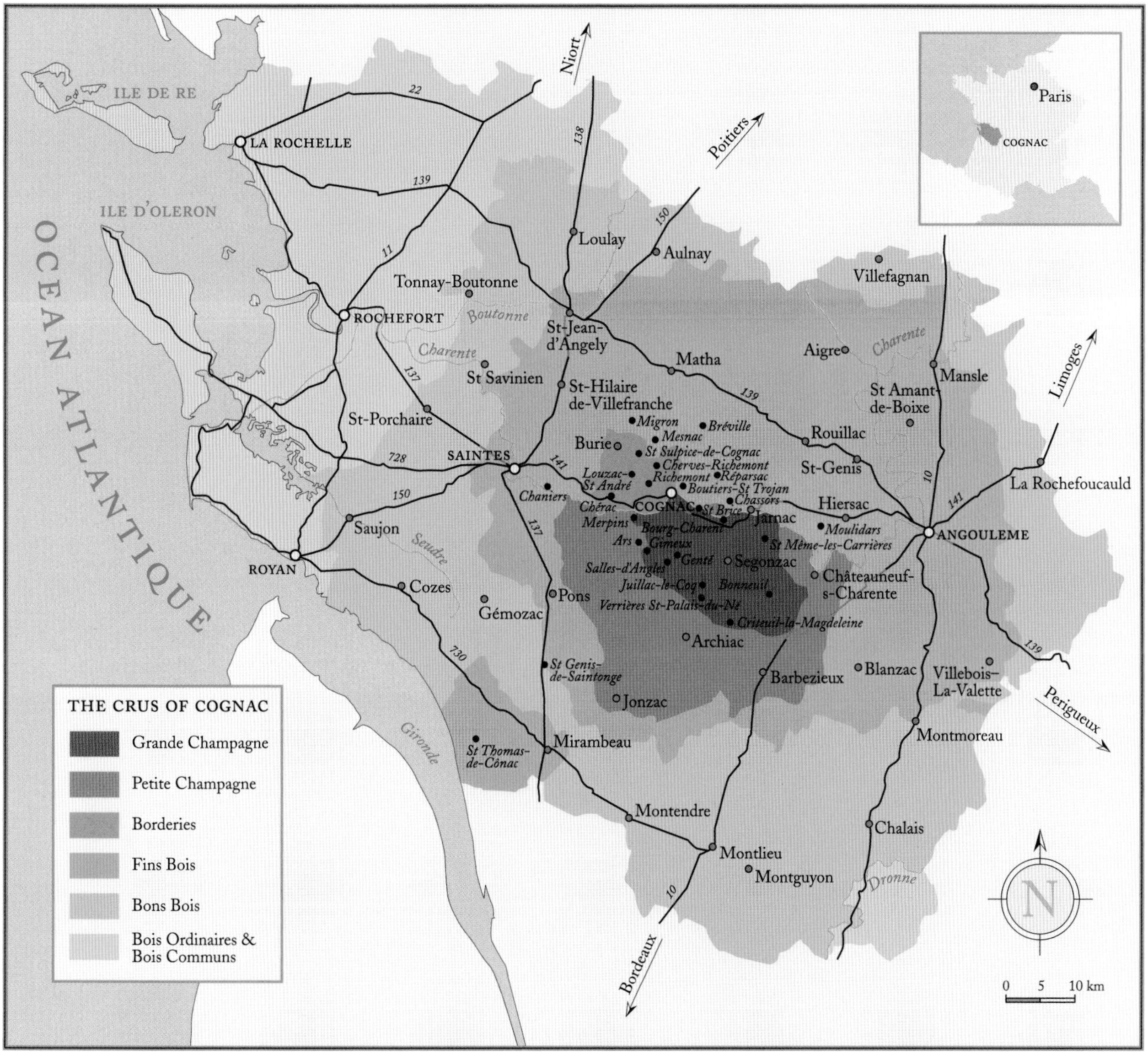

ABOVE: A MAP SHOWING THE SIX CRUS (REGIONS) WHERE GRAPES ARE GROWN TO PRODUCE THE EAU-DE-VIE THAT IS COGNAC.

Pausing for a moment, I could imagine the bustling scene as it might have been: cobbles alive with the sound of cartwheels crashing and whips cracking. Out of my reverie, I looked around, and couldn't help but notice the infamous black fungus, *Torula compniacensis richon*, that thrives on the fumes of cognac and reproduces itself easily. Guttering, rooftops, and walls of what were once white painted buildings were now dark with a fungal covering. Then the light aroma of cognac hit me as it wafted through the air – you could almost believe the angels have flitted by, leaving the aroma behind in their wake as they make off with the mystical 'angel's share' (*see* page 90/1).

I found the hotel, parked the car, and relaxed – I had reached the heart of Cognac country. Yet my journey was by no means complete, for over the next few days I would begin the task of talking to many of my friends, including Bernard Hine, Maurice Hennessy, Jean-Paul Camus and Jacques Rivière of A E Dor, about the current state of play regarding cognac.

PP14/5: THE RIVER CHARENTE IN FULL FLOW HAS A MURKY PAST OF CAPSIZED SHIPS, THEIR CARGO STILL HIDDEN DEEP IN THE MUDDY LAYERS BENEATH THE WAVES.

The town's residents live in a cycle that revolves around the production of cognac. For 365 days a year they care for the land and the vines, the grapes, and in October and November they begin harvesting. Winemaking and distillation continue until the end of March. Next, the cognac has to age in the cask, be tested continually by the master blender, whose art changes the *eau-de-vie* in the cask into a fine cognac, and then they wait. And wait.

'To make cognac, you must be patient,' remarked Charles Braastad-Delamain wryly during my most recent visit. He was right. Sometimes the wait can be for up to 50 years. After all, this is a spirit that cannot be rushed. At the end of that time there is a cask of 50-year-old cognac that is passed down from one generation to another. Thus, producing cognac is a long-term investment with no quick-and-easy cash flow. The cask is the tangible asset of an investment made by the family all those years ago. Indeed, you cannot make a fine cognac such as a *Paradis* or a *Reserve de la Famille* without a drop of a cognac like that.

The business has been resilient through both the phylloxera plague and through periods of low yield, such as during both world wars. There have also been the extremely successful years, particularly when the Asian market was booming. Talk to local people and they will remark that the town used to be wealthier back in the 1980s, before the world's finance markets were destabilized. Cognac is not isolated from world affairs. For instance, the 1996/97 stockmarket crash and currency crisis in Asia deeply affected the economy of the region. It is also affected by the world's currency markets, since over 91.8 per cent is exported to the rest of Europe, the United States of America and Asia.

The vineyards are currently once again in over-production, and the French government is talking to winegrowers about ripping out the Ugni Blanc vines and replacing them with other grape varieties. This is heresy to some, salvation to other growers, and the debate will last for a while yet.

But I digress. When the opportunity arose to write this book, I saw it as a challenge to pass on to anyone even slightly intrigued by the golden liquid as much of my passion for cognac as I could.

This is first and foremost a book about cognac as a liquid history. I have returned to learn more about cognac, since this obsession of mine is a neverending journey. I wonder if I will ever know everything about this mysterious *eau-de-vie*? For instance, when I walked into the cellar at Hine,

Bernard Hine stopped and smiled at me. 'You are an expert on cognac,' he said. 'Tell me: why is this chalky gravel on the ground under the casks?' He stood waiting for my reply. And for once, I was lost for words. I did not know.

He smiled again. 'The gravel is used to absorb the humidity of the ground and release it into the air. This humidity regulation is fantastic for providing a regular ageing to the cognac and giving it this mellow and smooth aroma.'

So I had learned something from the master, one of the greatest 'noses', and the last of the Hine generation still (at that time) working in the family business.

One of the purposes of this book is to explore the spirit of cognac itself, to present the background to some of the leading families and cognac houses in the business and region. I have tried to tell the personal stories, the tales you may not have read in other books on cognac. What I will not be doing is presenting an A to Z of every cognac house (there are over 250 after all). I have also attempted to present my view of both its economic and taste history, for over the last 130 years the new grape varieties planted throughout the region since the phylloxera disaster have been responsible for a different flavour and style of cognac.

I present a summary of the distillation process (cognac is distilled twice), and the importance of the oak cask, the move from cask to bottle, the associated development of labelling and branding, of modern marketing strategy, of the battle between cognac and other spirits.

The second part of the book deals with my deep and unabiding passion: vintage cognac. Here you will find tasting notes for my favourite vintage years, plus some amusing anecdotes about some of the people I have met while searching for rare bottles to add to my collection.

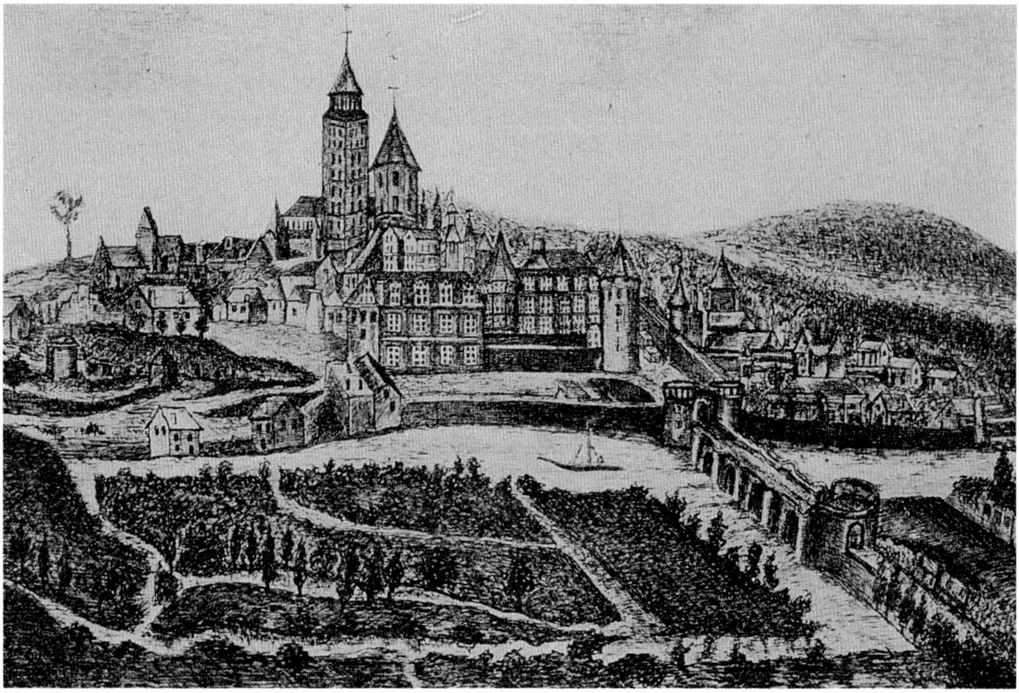

ABOVE: A VIEW OF THE TOWN OF COGNAC IN THE 15TH CENTURY BASED ON AN ANCIENT ENGRAVING.

You can also read tasting notes of some of the product range from a selection of the more familiar cognac houses whose bottles are available in most countries. There is no point in telling you about a smooth and undeniably great cognac if you cannot buy it, so, if the brand you prefer is not listed there, please accept my apologies in advance.

For me, too, this book has been a revelation. I rekindled my acquaintance with dear friends, made a few new ones, and on the journey added to my knowledge of the 'noble spirit'. I have come to the conclusion that the spirit of cognac will not die; an imaginatively designed bottle will always be part of the bartender's top shelf, and will be at home in any private bar collection.

Trends in drink come and go, but a classic drink is here forever, and cognac is a classic, no matter how you drink it.

And if I can persuade you, through the pages of this book, to explore the variety of taste experiences that cognac offers, then my journey has been worthwhile.

Enjoy!

Salvatore Calabrese

ABOVE: NAPOLEON BECAME THE NAME ON EVERYBODY'S LIPS AFTER COURVOISIER NAMED ITS COGNAC AFTER THE FRENCH GENERAL.

London Robt & Thos Harrison & Co

£ 1437 9 1 ... at 2 usance which doubt not will be honoured

130

£ 1567 9 1

Bordeaux Macarthy Freres

Nous vous confirmons notre ... 18 Court. & ... nous ...

portant l'extrait de votre compte chez vous pour balance duquel il ...

a quoi nous ... pour nous y complaisant vous ... accuser par ...

remettant Lt. ... 6 Rieff & Co. 1 May a Usance sur ...

£ 852 12 — ffs notre Lt. de ce jour 182 a 2 Usances notre ...

£ 150 — ffs

vous prions de placer au mieux de notre avantage & d'avoir la co...

de l'agio notre traite sur vous de ce jour

£ 644 16 — a 1 jour de date ordre S. Gautier.

Le temps s'est ici comme chez vous infiniment mal compo...

deja de beaucoup de dommage, mais il paroitra mieux aux ...

aux vendeurs ou acheteurs, il ne se fait rien & l'on ne peu...

Paris Mallet Pere Fils & Co

Nous vous confirmons notre derniere 11 Court. & ...

date promettant accueil a nos traites sur vous, mention...

votre complaisance d'avoir remis notre incluse a Mr S...

recommandant de nouvelle celles sous ce pli pour ...

Rochefort Lacoutomme.

L'honneur de votre lettre 23 Court. nous porte le ...

Lindsay & voyons que vous avez malgré notre ...

... d'une pareille qualité nous vous ...

... [illegible] lettre de notre ...

1

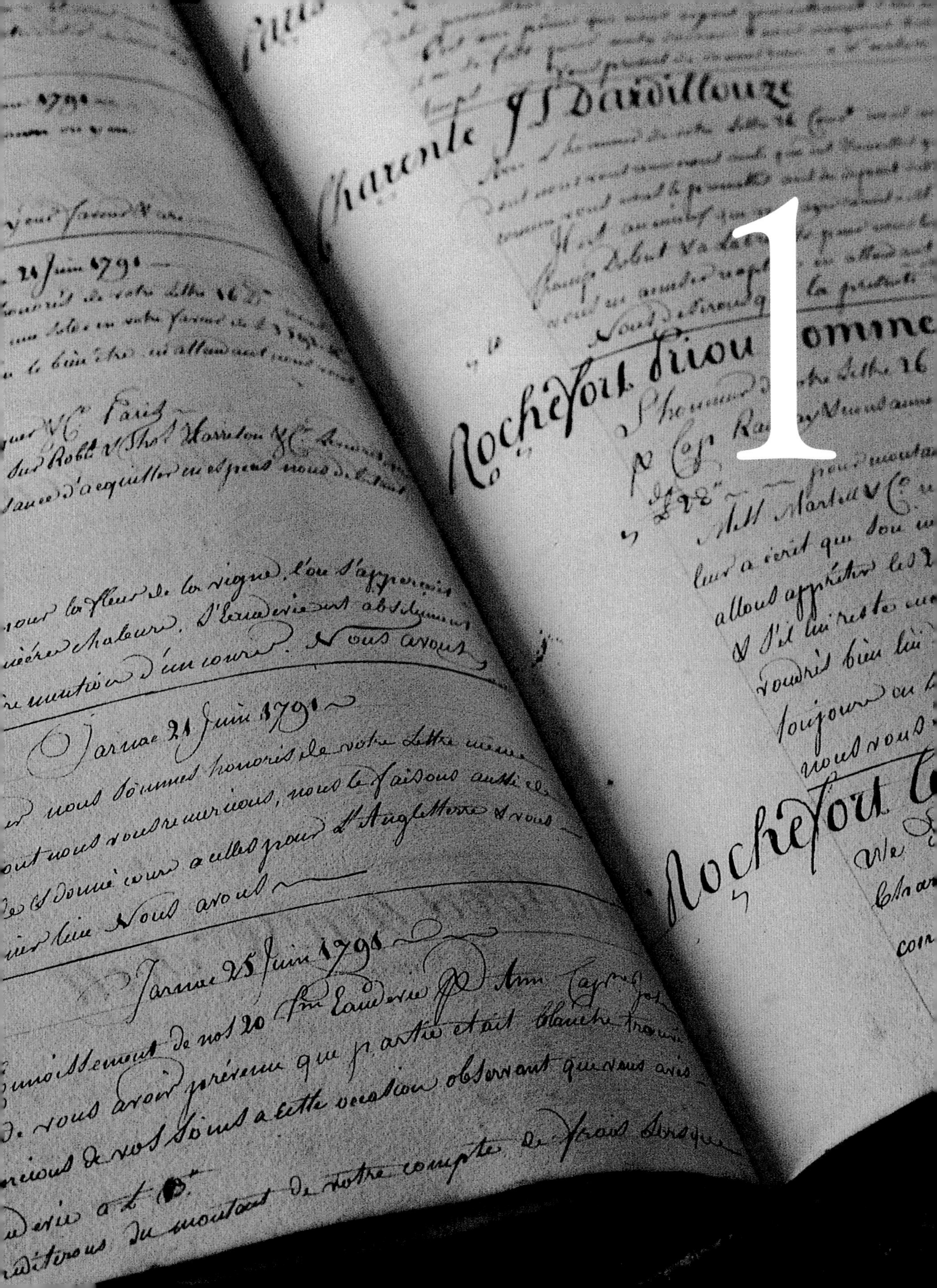

A SHORT TALE OF COGNAC

BC

circa 50BC	Julius Caesar takes control of Gaul, including what is today's Cognac country, the Charente-Maritime and Charente *départements*, which included the ancient province of Saintonge.

AD

92	Emperor Domitian bans the planting of vineyards in Gaul. Many vines in the provinces are grubbed up.
280	Emperor Probus repeals Domitian's ban; vineyard plantings begin again in Gaul.
circa 407	Vandals begin invasion of the Roman Empire.
400-410	Visigoths invade Roman Empire. Led by Alaric, they sack Rome for three days in August of 410.
430	Salt exported to the Northern countries from La Rochelle.
circa 480	The Franks arrive in the Saintonge province.
700-749	Saracen (Moorish) empire expands from Lisbon, Portugal, to China. The word alcohol, Arabic in origin, enters Europe, a corruption of *al khol* or *al kuhl*, which referred to black eye makeup derived from distillation.
721-804	The Arab Jabir promotes the art of distillation in Arabia.
732	Charles Martel defeats the Moors at the Battle of Tours, halting Arab invasion in Europe.
863	The Vikings (Norsemen) row up the flow of the River Charente.
early 11th C	Arab physician and philosopher Avicenna writes a treatise on distillation.

PP23/4: PAGES FROM A HINE JOURNAL DATING BACK TO THE FRENCH REVOLUTION, WITH ENTRIES SHOWING THE SALES OF COGNAC TO SHIPPERS.

1066	Norman Conquest of England begins.
1152	Wedding of Aliénor of Aquitaine and Henry Plantagenet, Duke of Normandy and Count of Anjou. In 1154, they become King Henry II and Queen Eleanor of England.
1171	Henry II of England becomes Lord of Ireland. English forces find Irish drinking *usque-baugh* – Gaelic term for 'water of life' and root of modern word 'whisky'.
1198	Wines of Saintonge province sold to the Flemish, according to the monk Renier de Saint-Jacques.
early 13th c	Arab scientists mention distilling alcohol, using an *anbîq*, a primative still.
1203	Philip II (Augustus) of France confiscates the Saintonge province from King John of England.
1242	Louis IX ('Saint') of France forces British to flee the Saintonge province.
1270	Frapin family established in the Charente region.
1300	First recipe for distilling wine in an *alembic* still appears.
mid-13th c	Thaddeus of Florence, founder of Bologna medical school, publishes book on distillates: *De Virtue Aquae Vitae, quae etiam dicitur aqua ardens* ('Concerning the Qualities of the Waters of Life, which is also named fiery water').
1337	The Hundred Years' War between France and England begins.
1337-1410	London receives still wines from Saintonge.
1356	John II ('The Good') of France is captured by the English at Poitiers.
1360	Treaty of Brètigny. The King of England renounces the crown of France.
early 14th c	Arnaldus da Villanova, professor of medicine at Montpellier University, publishes first-ever wine book, *Liber de Vinis*, in which he prescribes some *aqua vitae* for medicinal use.
1411	Armagnac is made for local consumption.
1453	Hundred Years' War ends. Charles VII enters Bordeaux.
1492	Christopher Columbus sets sail for the New World.
1493	Birth of Paracelsus, Swiss physician who uses a holistic approach to medicine. During his career, he experiments with distillation.
1494	Birth of King Francis I in Cognac (September 12th).
1494	First mention of distilling in Scotland. Scotch whisky is officially born.
1519	Alsace army surgeon Hieronymus Brunschwig publishes *Das Buch zu Destillieren (The Book of Distillation)*, in which he recommends *aqua vitae composita*, a mixture of Gascony wine, herbs and brandy.
1532	Religious Reformer John Calvin arrives in Angoumois.
1535	Henry VIII excommunicated. The Reformation begins.

1549	Shipment of brandy from La Rochelle recorded.
1556	Charles IX of France passes edict which limits planting of vineyards in the Cognac region.
1561	French religious wars begin with massacre of Huguenots at Vassy.
1573	Drought produces a scarcity of wine and corn in Angoumois.
1576	The French historian J Corlieu writes highly of the 'Champagne Charentaise'.
1579	The Dutch provinces become known as 'The Haulier of the Seas'.
1589	Henry IV becomes King of France after 40 years of civil war.
1598	Edict of Nantes provides freedom of worship for Protestants (Huguenots).
1617	Two hundreds barrels of the spirit of cognac are sold by a François Bertrand, a merchant of Tonnay-Charente, on the quayside.
1624	Two Dutchmen, Van Der Boogvert and Loo Dewijck, create a distillery at Tonnay-Charente.
1636	Revolt of the 'Clod-hoppers' against the French wine tax.
1637	Louis XIII establishes through trading dues the occupation of 'distillers making brandy'.
1638	English traveller Lewes Roberts mentions 'a small wine called Rotchell, but more properly Cogniacke'.
1643	Philippe Augier founds Cognac Augier.
1658	Augier Frères founded.
1678	*The London Gazette* mentions 'cogniack brandy'.
1679	English government bans all French wines. Louis XIV's minister Colbert takes opportunity to revoke the centuries-old *police des vins*, ensuring more commercial freedom for all French distillers and vintners.
1685	Louis XIV revokes the Edict of Nantes.
1688	The Glorious Revolution in England. James II deposed; marriage of Mary II to William of Orange.
1697	Frapin coat of arms awarded by Louis XIV.
1705	One barrel of spirit brandy costs £37.
1709	A harsh winter ruins the vineyards of Saintonge province.
1710	Claude Masse, French historian and writer, attributes the double-distillation process to an unknown chemist in La Rochelle.
1714	Wedding of Paul-Emile Rémy Martin to Marie Geay (January 19th).
1715	Jean Martell, from the island of Jersey, establishes Martell in Cognac.
1724	Paul-Emile Rémy Martin and Jean Geay (his father-in-law) establish Rémy Martin.

ABOVE: A PORTRAIT OF RICHARD HENNESSY IN ALL OF HIS FINERY PAINTED IN THE SECOND HALF OF THE 1700S.

1725	Isaac Ranson established a company in Jarnac to ship cognac to Holland and Ireland.
1726	French historian Gervais notes: 'The cognac brandy is considered as the best one of the world.'
1731	Louis XV forbids the planting of a vineyard without permission (June 5th).
1738	Louis XV grants Rémy Martin a licence to expand his vineyards because of the fine quality of his Cognac.
1753	Richard Hennessy becomes an officer in the Irish Brigade of Louis XV.
1756	Seven Years' War begins between England and France (French and Indian War in the American colonies).
1762	James Delamain becomes partner in Ransom & Delamain in Jarnac.
1763	James Delamain married Marie Ransom.
1765	Richard Hennessy founds Hennessy Cognac, moving to Cognac from Bordeaux.
1773	The Boston Tea Party takes place in Massachusetts colony, when the tea cargo of three English ships is destroyed in Boston harbour.
1775	The American Revolution begins with the Battle of Lexington and Concord.
1776	The Declaration of Independence is signed on July 4th. The United States of America is established.
1779	Ten cognac merchants established in Cognac town square, including Augier, Gautier, Martell, Hennessy and Rémy Martin.
1783	Peace of Paris ends American Revolution; Britain recognizes American independence. Bureau des Formes (Department of Conventions established in Cognac to monitor movement of *eau-de-vie*.
1784	Martell's first shipment of cognac to North America. Royal edict frees *eau-de-vie* from duty if destined for export.
1788	*The Times* newspaper first published in England.
1789	French Revolution begins.
1791	*Négociants* commit themselves to selling only high-quality 'Brandy of Saintonge'.
1793	The 'Reign of Terror' begins in France. All English ships on the Charente are seized. Whisky makes inroads into the established cognac market.
1794	Hennessy sends its first shipment to New York.
1795	Baron Jean-Baptiste Antoine Otard and Jean Dupuy establish Cognac Otard. James Hennessy marries Marthe Martell.
1796	First shipment of 'spirit brandy' from Cognac to Prussia and Sweden.
1797	Wedding of Thomas Hine and Elizabeth Delamain.

1801	United Kingdom of Great Britain and Ireland established.
1804	Napoléon becomes Emperor of France.
1805	Battle of Trafalgar.
1806	Continental blockade imposed by Napoléon has devastating effect on cognac trade.
1815	Napoléon defeated by Wellington at Battle of Waterloo.
1817	Creation of Thomas Hine & Co.
1817	First appearance of the appellation VOP (Very Old Pale) and VSOP (Very Superior Old Pale).
1819	Alexandre Bisquit establishes Cognac Bisquit.
1824	Henri Delamain joins his cousin Paul Roullet in Jarnac to establish Roullet & Delamain.
1831	First delivery of Martell VSOP to London.
1833	Shipment of a first barrel of Pineau de Charente to King Louis-Philippe.
1835	Fèlix Courvoisier and Louis Gallois establish Courvoisier in Jarnac.
1838	Creation of the Cooperative-Society of Owners of wine producers in Cognac.
1847	First sale of 100 cases of Old Pale cognac in bottles by Denis-Mounié (11 per cent of the shipments).
1849	Martell puts first labels on bottles of cognac. California Gold Rush begins. Cut in taxes on brandy spirits in England.
1850	First shipment of cognac to Australia.
1852	Louis-Napoléon proclaims himself Napoléon III ('Second Empire').
1854	Map of the cognac vineyard regions appears, showing four *crus*: Grande Champagne, Petite Champagne, Premier Bois and Deuxième Bois.
1855	Hennessy bottle produced by the Poilly Brigode Company at Folembray Glass Works.
1856	First labels of Jas Hennessy & Cie appear on bottles.
1857	Law enabling registration of commercial brands passed.
1858	Creation of the first trademark on the casks made by branding. A E Dor established in Jarnac.
1859	Competition in St Louis, Missouri (United States) sets out quality of Cognacs. First shipments of Cognac to Calcutta, India.
1860	Treaty of Free Trade signed by Michel Chevalier (France) and Richard Cobden (England).
1861	Martell's first shipment to China. American Civil War begins.
1863	Jean-Baptiste Camus establishes Camus.

1864	Hennessy registers brand names and axe-in-hand logo.
1865	Auguste Hennessy creates the star-rating system for Cognac. American Civil War ends.
1869	Opening of the Suez Canal.
1870	Second map of region shows six *crus* with the addition of Fins Bois and Bons Bois regions. Hennessy records deposit at the Cognac clerk's office of the acronym XO (Extra Old). Franco-Prussian War begins. First shipments to Bombay, India.
1872	Phylloxera appears in Crouin, Charente and in Chérac in the Charente-Maritime region. Begins its destruction of the Saintongeais vineyards. Whisky starts its takeover of cognac's share of spirit market.
1872	Arrival of five cases of Hennessy XO at Shanghai.
1873	Napoléon III (Louis-Napoléon) dies.
1875	Cognac house Tiffon founded on the quayside in Jarnac
1876	The first label appears on a bottle of Courvoisier.
1877	The Cognac vineyard extends over 282,667 hectares (ha).
1878	Claude Boucher buys the Faubourg Saint-Martin glassworks in cognac.
1881	Dr Richon, a respected mycologist, classifies *Torula compniacensis richon*. Claude Boucher patents a bottle-moulding process.
1882	Production of *eau-de-vie* reaches 1,724,232 hectolitres (hl).
1883	Hennessy third best-selling Cognac.
1885	Hennessy ranked fourth, behind Courvoisier. First degree of merit awarded to Pierre Frapin at New Orléans World Fair.
1888	Phylloxera-resistant grafting stock brought in from Dennison, Texas to replant cognac vineyards.
1889	Cognac production equals just 307,758 hl. Exposition de Paris: Courvoisier and Frapin receive gold medals.
1890	Hennessy ranks number one in cognac sales. Charente vineyards cover just 46,000 ha as opposed to 285,000 in 1896.
1891	Madrid Convention discusses international protection of spirit trademarks.
1892	Viticultural research laboratory established in Cognac, headed by Professor Louis Ravaz.
1895	12,000 ha of vineyards are replanted using American rootstocks.
1899	Decline in trade with Great Britain.
1900	Commerical rivalry between Martell and Hennessy becomes intense.
1904	World Trade Fair in St Louis, Missouri (United States) defends the use of a label guaranteeing the quality of cognac.

ABOVE: FORMER SMUGGLER JEAN MARTELL WAS A SIGNIFICANT FORCE IN THE DEVELOPMENT OF TRADE BETWEEN COGNAC AND EUROPE, AMERICA AND THE FAR EAST.

1909	Six *crus* of the Cognac region are defined and protected by law.
1910	André Renaud becomes associate in Emile Rémy Martin, a new company with its head office in Cognac.
1912	Martell creates Cordon Bleu label.
1914	First World War begins. Cognac made during 1914 becomes known as 'The Year of the Lady' since the men had all gone to fight in the First World War (1914 to 1918).
1918	Russian market closes.
1919	The Volstead Act: 18th Amendment ratified; Prohibition begins in the United States. Courvoisier invents 'The Brandy of Napoléon'.
1921	Quebec and the British Columbia create licence system controlling the sale of alcohol by the government, followed by Manitoba in 1923, Alberta in 1924 and Ontario in 1927.
1923	Hennessy and Martell sign agreement regarding territories and sharing of information to last 29 years.
1924	André Renaud takes over Rémy Martin.
1927	The words 'Fine Champagne' appear on a bottle of Rémy Martin VSOP.
1929	*Acquit jaune d'Or* certificate sets cognac apart from other wines. The stock market in the United States collapses; the Depression begins. St Valentine's Day Massacre, Chicago, Illinois (United States).
1930	Cognac becomes a fashionable cocktail.
1931	Foundation of UNICOOP, an association of vine-growers, in Cognac. Devaluation of the British pound. Exports to Great Britain rise.
1933	December: Prohibition repealed.
1934	The appearance of the shadow of Napoléon in Courvoisier's advertisements.
1936	Gaston Briand and Robert Delamain take part in the mapping of Cognac vineyards. Cognac vineyards must be composed exclusively of white grape varieties, addition of sugar is prohibited; the term *fine* is authorized by law to describe an *appellation d'origine contrôlée eau-de-vie*.
1937	Two hundred American spirit merchants visit Cognac.
1939	Second World War begins.
1940	France occupied by the Germans. Bureau de Repartition des Vins et Eaux-de-Vie established. Stocks taken by occupying troops total 8,446,000 bottles out of a total despatch of 41,570,000 bottles.
1941	Creation of the National Office of Distribution for wine and *eau-de-vie* of Cognac. Bombing of Pearl Harbour by the Japanese; the United States enters the war.

1944	D-Day in Normandy.
1945	VE Day. A late frost reduces harvest to 24,000 hl.
1946	Creation of the Bureau National Interprofessionnel du Cognac.
1949	People's Republic of China bans all imports.
1951	The St Bernard, with a small cask of Hennessy around its neck, becomes advertising feature in the United States.
1953	Coronation of Elizabeth II in England.
1957	Treaty of Rome established the European Economic Community. Reduction in duties has immediate effect on Cognac sales.
1962	Hine granted a British Royal Warrant.
1963	Assassination of John F Kennedy, President of the United States.
1964	Courvoisier bought by Canadian Hiram-Walker group.
1967	Cognac Bisquit is purchased by the French group Pernod-Ricard.
1969	United States lands first man on the moon.
1971	Merger between Hennessy and Moët & Chandon. Thomas Hine is bought by The Distillers Company Limited.
1974	Fire at Martell warehouse destroys 12,000 barrels of Cognac.
1975	Martell is floated on the Parisian stock exchange.
1984	*The start of my passion (Salvatore Calabrese).*
1986	Courvoisier bought by Allied Domecq.
1987	Creation of Louis-Vuitton-Moët-Hennessy (LVMH). Thomas Hine et Cie becomes part of Hennessy after LVMH buys the company from Guinness.
1988	Martell purchased by Seagram.
1990	Rémy Martin and Scottish company Highland Distillers sign a trade agreement. Dominique Hèriard-Dubreuil named Prèsident of Rémy Martin.
1991	Deep frosts over the Charentais vineyards.
1992	Martell begins sponsorship of England's Grand National horse-race.
1993	Cognac vineyards cover 87,313 ha across all *crus*.
1998	Dominique Hèriard-Dubreuil appointed chairwoman of Rémy-Cointreau, the spirits conglomerate her father envisaged. Angry vine-growers block Jarnac's roads in protest at problems of the cognac industry.
1999	Rémy-Cointreau, Highland Distillers, and Jim Beam Brands form a worldwide distribution joint venture excluding the United States.
2001	United States drinks giant Seagram (including Martell) purchased by Pernod-Ricard and Diageo.

ROYALTY, PRIVILEGE & TAXATION

'Making great cognac is easy. All you need is a great-grandfather and a father who have dedicated their lives to it.'

JEAN-PAUL CAMUS

TO TELL THE EARLY HISTORY OF COGNAC MEANS TRAVELLING BACK IN TIME TO WHEN THE ROMAN EMPEROR JULIUS CAESAR CONQUERED GAUL.

Being Italian, I am exhilarated that my passion for cognac has led me to the land my countrymen once walked upon. The part they played in the development of cognac is small but integral. As with many things, to understand the present, it is important to understand past associations of people and politics. Cognac's history is beset with intrigue, religious wars, and abduction.

PP34/35: IN THE HEART OF GRANDE CHAMPAGNE STANDS THIS RUIN OF A 12TH CENTURY CHATEAU.

Although, in all probability, the creation of the cognac spirit did not take place until the 17th century, the Romans had instigated the activity of winemaking in the Cognac region in ancient times, when they brought their knowledge of viticulture to France. Roman ruins discovered near Saintes, between Cognac and the Atlantic coast, reveal designs of grapes and grape leaves in ancient carvings. However, there is no historical evidence that there were ever vineyards planted during this early period in the old provinces that once covered the territory now known as the Charente and Charente-Maritime *départements*.

Both the Charente and Charente-Maritime were once ancient provinces called Aunis, Saintogne and Angoumois, through which flowed the River

Charente, called by King Henry IV 'the loveliest stream in my kingdom'. Many French writers refer to it as the *molle* – soft and sweet; it is a magnificent stretch of water that meanders at will on its journey to the seaport of La Rochelle on the northwest coast, where it merges with the Atlantic Ocean.

Bordered by willow trees sweeping their branches in the river as it passes by, the Charente has yet to reveal the secrets it keeps about trading ships wrecked and settled in its muddy depths. In their holds are crates containing bottles of what are almost certainly vintage cognacs, untouched since they reached their murky graveyard. That morbid image aside, the Charente today is a landscape to envy. Floating upriver in the afternoon, past fields of corn wafting in the light, late-summer breeze, it is easy to imagine why the town of Cognac was built on its banks some 2,000 years ago. The town's location on the Charente has been partly responsible for its commercial success. The ease of transport along the river augered well for its inhabitants in a period when exploration and trading were of paramount importance.

Further south lies Bordeaux, important because of its strategic seaport position. Like many wealthy Roman settlements, it was busy with traders. Rome was keen to protect and promote its commercial interests in cities such as Bordeaux, but due to a glut of wine caused by large-scale random planting in the early 1st century, the emperor Domitian decreed in AD92 that no vineyards were to be planted, no wine produced or exported north of the River Gironde, which included the Charente Valley.

It is well documented that the Roman emperor Probus, toward the end of the 3rd century AD, overturned Domitian's decree and granted all Gallic people the right to plant vineyards and make wine. The temperate climate, its chalky soil, the growers' affinity with the *terroir*, and the existence of the river combined to make the Cognac region one of the most important areas for wine production. Wine from the Saintonge and its sister provinces was exported via the river to other regions in France and the Roman Empire.

After the fall of the Roman Empire, the Cognac region descended into a form of chaos, occupied by one foreign power or another until around the 10th century, when the town of Cognac was fortified by the first 'lord' of Cognac, Monsieur Hélie de Villebois. The town's name is thought to come from that of a Gaulish chieftain, *Comnos* or *Conos*. Villebois recognized the strategic importance of the town on the river, that it was a crossroads on the axis of the Charente linking Limousin and the sea, near the threshold of Poitou and the estuary of the Gironde. He was also responsible for building one of the first chateaux on the left bank of the river. Alas, there is no sign of it today.

The river was also being used to transport another vital commodity from the region: salt. Known as 'white gold', salt was extracted from seawater in the area around La Rochelle, at the mouth of the Charente River on the Atlantic coast, and traded as a basic necessity for the preservation of meat and fish during the long winter; it was also an essential as part of any ship's stores. The *gabelle*, or salt tax, imposed by the government, was an important source of revenue for the region. Wander through the old town in Cognac and you will come across rue Saulnier, or 'Street of the Salt Harbour', where stands the Maison de la Gabelle, once the centre for the salt-tax collection; these days, it is yet another brandy warehouse in a town full of buildings recycled as warehouses.

Traders from northern Europe, including Flanders, Scandinavia and Germany, thought the salt from around La Rochelle among the best available.

Also, from a purely commercial pont of view, it was cheaper for the shippers to pay a 20-per cent tax on the salt traded in the Angoumois provence, which encompassed La Rochelle, than to pay a 25-per cent tax in either the Saintogne or Aunis provinces. In modern commercial terms, this would be seen as undercutting the competition and probably would be outlawed by the European Union. In those days, however, it was just business as usual.

During the Middle Ages, from the 12th to the mid-15th centuries, the English and the French took it in (irregular) turns to rule parts of France. In 1120, Charente was part of the duchy of Duke William X of Aquitaine. The duke's official residence was located in Bordeaux, yet he often lived in the town of La Rochelle. Under his vision and drive, La Rochelle became the most important trading port in western France.

In fact, the entire region flourished under William's rule, and it attracted settlers from many parts of Europe, keen to exploit the relatively mild climate. It was a heyday for both vintners and merchants; they were successfully trading with the Vikings, the Scots and the Moorish rulers of Andalusia.

William's heir was his daughter Aliénor, or Eleanor, of Aquitaine. Hers was an influential life. Her first marriage to King Louis VII of France was followed by her second to Henry II, Duke of Normandy and Count of Anjou, in 1152. In 1154, Henry and Eleanor became king and queen of England. Henry ruled the Aunis and Saintogne provinces as Duke of Guyenne and the Count of Poitiers from 1152 to 1189.

Eleanor's marriage provided new and important commercial opportunities for the merchants of Cognac, both in Paris and across the English Channel in London. While Henry ruled over an Anglo-French empire for 34 years, the

English upper classes developed a taste for the new wave of wines being produced in the *vignoble de Poitou*. As duke, Henry encouraged the planting of vineyards in the Poitou area, recognizing the special qualities of its *terroir*, and hoping that they would satisfy the demands of the English and Flemish merchants seeking quality wines for their home markets. Vine cultivation became the basis of the Charentais economy.

The Musée du Cognac's history of the region contains a declaration, made in 1198 by the monk Renier de Saint-Jacques, that for the first time, some wine from La Rochelle was delivered to Liège, in modern-day Belgium – a place where, previously, only wines originating from Germany's Rhine or Moselle regions had been available. This document also shows the expansion of Charentais exports into Flanders, via the port of Damme (Bruges' outer harbour), and also through other Flemish coastal ports.

PP40/1: THE SHUTTERED STREETS OF COGNAC WIND THEIR WAY FROM THE SQUARE TO THE QUAYSIDE OF THE RIVER CHARENTE.

Other documents reveal the manner in which business was done in the Rochelais vineyard region during the 13th century. A farmer would ask his landowner to grant him a plot of land while he, in return, pledged to plant it with vines. The landowner gave him full control of the land for five years, after which time the vineyard was divided into two equal parts: one returned to the landowner, the other remained with the tenant for an annual fee. Thus these vineyards produced wines for trading to North Sea countries, delivered there by Dutch and Scandinavian ships. La Rochelle wines were also popular in Paris, due to easy access to this city via the River Seine.

The Musée du Cognac's archives hold far fewer files on the Saintogne vineyards of the same period. What has been clearly established is that, in 1214, the English King John (Henry VII's heir) abducted and married Isabelle Taillefer, daughter of the Earl of Angoulême. He also negotiated with members of the Cognac industrial tribunal to buy wine for him.

Trade from the Aunis and Saintogne provinces expanded mainly into Flanders and England, through political allegiances and familiarity with the trading ships' routes. During this time, the Flemish abolished duty on wine; six years after this, around 1337, the Earl of Flanders granted special privileges to merchants who had their wine delivered to the Damme warehouses. An improved trading situation encouraged wine production in the Charente basin, and the vineyard region was extended inland.

King John granted special privileges to Cognac, giving the town economic and politcal freedom. Then, in the 14th century, it became separated from the usual feudal system that ruled the rest of France. Even the neighbouring town of Jarnac, just 15 kilometres away, was not granted the same advantages – one possible reason why brandy from this region was not called *Jarnac*, despite the fact that some of the well-known cognac houses today are based in Jarnac.

Until the end of the Hundred Years' War in the mid-1400s, the English ruled most of the western area of France. The French re-took the Charante region sooner than Bordeaux, which, out of loyalty to King John, was the last town to surrender. The return of French rule had far-reaching consequences. The Charentais lost access to their main market (England), and the vineyards saw constant battle action until almost the end of the conflict. Throughout this uncertain period, winemaking was not such a major economic factor as it had been previously. Some of the region's vineyards were uprooted, and in the Grande and Petite Champagne areas, land was sown with grain, not grapes.

In other areas, forests were planted. For this reason, Cognac's modern wine-growing areas are designated in accordance with these zones: Fins Bois, Bons Bois and Bois Communs.

One good outcome of the Hundred Years' War was that it forced local merchants – winemakers included – to source other markets; consequently, many turned to the countries which had bought salt in earlier centuries. The Cognaçais also sold their wines throughout France, thus setting up a home market decades in advance of the Bordeaux vintners.

The year 1494 proved auspicious for the people of Cognac, as the future King François I was born there. When he ascended to the throne some 23 years later, François exempted the people of his 'home town' from the taxes, loans and other levies forced upon the rest of the county of Angoulême to pay for the French army during its many skirmishes. The main reason for the king's generosity seems to have been his desire to see Cognac rewarded for its loyalty during the many sieges and battles fought in the Hundred Years' War. These privileges continued throughout the king's life, and in effect, created an environment that encouraged its inhabitants to feel 'protected' from the hardship others had to face.

Despite this protected status, peace had not yet been agreed in the region. In 1544, after the death of François I, traders revolted against the *gabelle* and were severely routed by royalist troops. This action added fuel to the smouldering Protestant (Huguenot) fire: followers of John Calvin heading for La Rochelle, a Huguenot stronghold, found refuge in the new forests around Angoulême on the Charante. The region gained a reputation as a safe refuge for fleeing Protestants and consequently was the site of many religious battles over the next 60 years, ending, for a time, with the Edict of Nantes in 1598.

ABOVE: FRANÇOIS I (1494–1547) WITH HIS FINE AQUILINE NOSE. HE WAS CONSIDERED A LADIES MAN IN HIS ERA.

Research undertaken by one of the region's leading historians, Pauline Reverchon, has led her to believe that the Charentais were already distilling some of their wine and exporting *eau-de-vie* – any fermented and distilled fruit spirit – as a single-distillation, unaged and rather rough brandy, at the start of the religious wars. The trade, she concluded, was expanded by the Huguenots, supported by their Protestant contacts in Amsterdam, London, and even the cities of Copenhagen and Hamburg. The Edict of Nantes, in effect, helped to secure these deals.

The main towns in the region, including Cognac, Jarnac, Segonzac and, nearer the coast, La Rochelle, were Calvinist strongholds, as were many of the families who developed the burgeoning trade, such as the Delamains and Hines of Jarnac, the Augiers and Martells of Cognac. Many of these families stayed behind during the Huguenot exodus that followed the revocation of the Edict of Nantes in 1685; some took up the Roman Catholic faith, and others remain Protestant to this day.

OPPOSITE: THE CROIX (CROSS) OF THE HOUSE OF CAMUS IS SET IN STONE AT THEIR HEADQUARTERS IN COGNAC.

The 17th century saw a change in fortune for the Charentais. Dutch traders came in search of the quality white wines grown in vineyards near Segonzac, and those of the Borderies: Javrezac, Saint-Laurent, Saint-André, Saint-Sulphice, Cherves, and Louzac. The English, Dutch and Scandinavian palates were very partial to the sweet, fragrant, sparkling wines made from the Colombard grape, the most prevelant vine planted in those regions.

The influence of the Dutch, British and Flemish traders was felt throughout the Charente Valley, and not always in a positive way. Some historians believe they encouraged the growth of common vines, to the detriment of the quality of

1863

the wines made from them. Documentary evidence from 1581 reveals that wines coming from La Rochelle were considered to be the worst-quality wines imported into Holland, and were sold at half the average price of good wines.

Being acidic and of low alcoholic strength, these wines might have suffered from the long sea trip. However, Dutch merchants turned this to their advantage, by distilling the wines. In the 17th century, wine from the Saintogne, the Aunis and the Angoumois regions was imported in an *eau-de-vie* form, which was then mixed with wines of other origins, and water. This mixture had another important role: to act as a purifier for the impure water that sailors carried during their long journeys at sea.

The first stills installed on the banks of the River Charente by the Dutch were gradually modified; the French developed and improved the technique by introducing double distillation. Hence the *eau-de-vie* no longer suffered from being shipped across long distances. More highly concentrated than wine, spirits are easier to transport. The resultant liquid became known as *brandywijn, brandvin, brandewijn* – the Dutch word for 'burnt wine'.

The 17th century also saw the foundation of the first cognac houses. Owing to the demand for the region's wines, *comptoirs* (agencies) were created in the main towns, some of which are still in existence. These agencies collected the cognac, sold and shipped it.

Augier Frères & Co was established in 1643, and the company was a force in the development of the cognac business over decades. The company of Godet are of Dutch origin, and settled in the coastal town of La Rochelle in 1600, shipping casks, not using their own name as a brand until later. Another house that has owned vineyards in the region since 1684 is that of J R Brillet.

Guy Brillet was born in 1656 and he chose his family estate, Bois d'Angeac, to locate his first distillery toward the end of the 17th century. The distillery was moved to Graves in 1850 by a descendant, Vivien Brillet. The brand is still in the family and has been run by a 10th generation member, Jean-Louis Brillet, since 1985.

Most of the cognac houses that we are familiar with today were established in the 18th century, as were the support industries: glass-making, wooden-case manufacturing and printing (for labels). So the region was comparatively undeveloped in a commercial sense in the 17th century, partly because of the instability of a century or more of wars being fought on the vast areas of fertile land that is now planted with vineyards.

This land, this *terroir*, holds the key to the success of the Charente region. There is an undefinable quality to cognac country that has compelled many writers and painters to wax lyrical of 'soft radiance' and 'tranquility', 'gently rolling country', 'a sun that shines under a soft, pearly sky' when describing the Charente region, and the most oft-used word is the French, '*douce*'. These are not for me, the words of observers past, although I recognise these qualities when visiting the region. There is nothing 'mild' about my passion and I have come to my own conclusion about Cognac and its *terroir*: it is simply the best place in the world a cognac-lover could ever wish to be.

WHAT LIES BENEATH

'Blending cognac is all a matter of taste. You can have a bouquet all of roses in a single cru like Grande Champagne, or a bouquet of a variety of flowers in a multiple crus cognac.'

PHILIPPE BRAASTAD-TIFFON

TO ME, COGNAC COULD NOT BE PRODUCED IN ANY OTHER AREA. THERE IS SOMETHING IN THE REGION'S TERROIR THAT PRODUCES A VERY COMPLEX SPIRIT, and so many factors affect its final colour, flavour and smell. Many of these are the result of the production and ageing processes after the grapes have been harvested, but equally, many have to do with the grapes themselves, which are influenced by where and how they are grown. Identical processes can be applied to the same grapes anywhere in the world, but it would be impossible to produce cognac anywhere other than in the region that bears its name. Here, *terroir* plays a role that cannot be ignored.

PP50/51: THE SUN FADES ON COGNAC'S HORIZON AND THE COUNTRYSIDE RESTS.
OPPOSITE: SOIL IS IMPORTANT IN COGNAC MAKING; MANY HOUSES NOW USE ORGANIC METHODS.

Legally, cognac can be produced only from grapes grown in the cognac *appellation contrôlée*, where the soil is generally chalky and the atmosphere maritime and cool, with local microclimates. These conditions produce a thin, sour, but intensely flavoured wine that is perfect for making brandy. The cognac *appellation* includes most of the Charente and Charente-Maritime *départements* north of the Gironde estuary, and the whole of the basin of the River Charente; it even includes some small islands in the Bay of Biscay. The River Charente runs through the middle of the region. Here, the cooler climates of the north

meet the hotter ones of the south. At the same time, the softer maritime weather from the coast meets its more continental cousin from inland France and Europe. This means that the area's general climate is temperate: not harsh in winter 6.5°C (42°F), and, although the days are long and hot in summer, the average is only 21.5°C (71°F). The result of this relatively mild summer is that the grapes do not become too ripe, and thus retain the acidity necessary for good cognac.

However, there are also existing odd pockets, or microclimates, that add their own influences to the grapes. The area towards the coast is moister and cooler, while further to the east, beyond the town of Cognac, the climate becomes harsher and more extreme.

The landscape varies from rolling hills to lowland plains, interspersed with green valleys and boggy marshland, open fields and woodland. The soil is generally chalky, becoming more sandy nearer the coast, but it also includes some clay and sand.

PP54/55: PRUNING IN THE LATE WINTER MONTHS IS CRUCIAL IN THE CYCLE OF VINEYARD MANAGEMENT. IT PREPARES THE VINE FOR A SPRING OUTBURST

The six *crus*, or vineyard regions, are arranged around the towns of Cognac and Jarnac in roughly concentric circles (*see* page 13). The total area in which cognac could be produced was defined in 1909, and in 1938, the six individual *crus* were legally designated; originally, there had been seven, but two were subsequently amalgamated. Although they relate roughly to soil types and to the quality of grapes they produce, there is some overlap among them. For example, the soil in a few small parts of the Petite Champagne area is close to that of the Grande Champagne, and produce almost the same quality cognac.

The two inner zones are known as *Champagnes*, meaning, in this instance, open fields. The *cru* immediately surrounding the town of Cognac is known as

La Grande Champagne, while the area that surrounds this on three sides is called La Petite Champagne. To the north lies the small Borderies region. Around this inner core is Les Fins Bois, which in turn is surrounded by Les Bons Bois. Finally, there is the area towards the coast known as the Les Bois à Terroir, more commonly called Les Bois Ordinaires. Together, the vineyards of the six Cognac *crus* constitute just about 80,000 hectares (ha).

The central Grande Champagne is considered the source of the finest cognacs. It is not so open to the mild maritime climate as the *crus* farther west, and its all-important soil, spread across gentle slopes, is composed mainly of a layer of Campanian chalk. Here, grapes gain a high acidity content and produce a fine, light, full-flavoured spirit with a predominantly floral bouquet. Grande Champagne cognac takes a long time of cask-ageing in order to reach full maturity. The *cru* encompasses 27 *communes*, or winemaking communities, and extends to a total area of 35,700 ha. Of this, 13,000 are planted with vines.

The Petite Champagne *cru* is almost twice the size of the Grande Champagne, covering 60 *communes* and 68,400 ha; however, only 16,000 of these are vineyards. While still chalky, the soil here is mainly Santonian chalk – more compact than the friable slopes of the Grande Champagne. This slight change in soil makes for a subtle difference in both the grapes which grow here and in the finished cognac distilled from them; while it is still extremely good cognac, it does not possess quite the same finesse as that made from grapes grown in the Grande Champagne; its bouquet is delicately floral. The weather in the western part of the Petite Champagne is influenced by the cooler weather coming off the Bay of Biscay, while on the other side, it is exposed to the climates of the Central Massif and the inland continent.

The Borderies region, situated to the north and west of the town of Cognac, is much smaller than the other *crus*. It includes just 10 *communes* and covers 13,440 ha, of which just 4,000 are devoted to vines. The soil here is a mixture of chalk and clay, and it has a microclimate all its own; grapes planted here ripen earlier than those in the other regions. The result of this early ripening is apparent in the Borderies cognacs, which are fine and rounded, smooth and offering an aroma of violets. They need much less time to reach final maturity in cask than that those from the two Champagne regions.

Around the central core of these three *crus*, but lying mainly to the north with an outcrop bordering on the River Gironde, is the Fins Bois. This extends to over 354,200 ha, with just under a tenth (33,000 ha) covered with vines. The soil here is chalk over a hard limestone subsoil, and tends to produce a round, supple cognac that matures quickly in 10 to 12 years, with a bouquet that recalls the smell of freshly pressed grapes.

Outside this is the Bon Bois, an even bigger area covering 386,600 ha, including 12,000 devoted to vines. Although the region boasts one small area of chalk, the soil is composed mainly of clay. The western section has a milder climate, as it is closer to the sea. cognac from here matures quickly, but is rougher in the mouth.

Finally, the Bois Ordinaire (Les Bois à Terroir) borders the sea and includes the islands of Oléron and Ré. An area of 274,176 ha – only 1,700 ha are planted with vines. The soil consists entirely of free-draining sand and the climate is maritime. Cognac from here is less subtle and usually described as having 'a characteristic local flavour' – a polite way of saying that it is the least interesting of the six *crus*.

ABOVE: WOMEN PICKED THE RIPENED GRAPES FOR CENTURIES. 1914 WAS HAILED 'LADIES VINTAGE'.

The first maps of the region (dated 1855, 1861 and 1875) were drawn up as a rationalization of a quality versus price structure. It was acknowledged that there was a difference in quality between cognacs from Grande Champagne and those from the three Bois; thus, sale prices differed. This relationship between region and quality remained the rationale behind legislation in the 19th and 20th centuries.

Today, merchants are allowed by law to market their cognacs under the name of the district of origin of *eau-de-vie* as a controlled *appellation*. Cognac labels are also allowed to bear the appellation 'Fine Champagne', if the cognac, a blend of Grande and Petite Champagne, contains at least 50 per cent spirit derived from grapes within the Grande Champagne region.

In addition to their impact on grapes, soil and climate influence other aspects of cognac production. The Limousin and Tronçais regions, for example, are perfect for growing oak for cask-making: their straight trees have an open-grained texture and just the right degree of tannins and lignins for maturing cognac (*see* Chapter 3). Similarly, the best cellars for maturing cognac are found on the banks of the Charente, where the moist atmosphere creates just the right degree of humidity – crucial to the amount of spirit, known romantically as the 'angel's share', that evaporates from the casks.

PP60/61: A FARMYARD SCENE IN A TYPICAL CHARENTAIS VINEYARD REVEALS SELF-SUFFICIENCY.

Many a *maître de chai* (cellar-master) has spent a lifetime trying to work out the subtle magic of the chemical process that involves newly distilled liquid, the pores of a solid-oak cask, the humidity in a darkened cellar and the weather outside. Each has his own theories, but most will admit that what goes on inside the cask is still an enigmatic mystery.

ABOVE: SMALL VINEYARDS WERE RUN ON A MANUAL PRODUCTION LINE BACK IN 1900.

CREATION OF A GOLDEN LIQUID

'I realised the impact of carrying the Martell name when I started to travel. For example, in America. It's a new country and you say my family dates from 1750, and they say to you you're older than America.'

LAUREN MARTELL

ONE OF THE MOST IMPORTANT TIMES TO BE IN COGNAC, IF YOU ARE AS FASCINATED AS I AM BY THE MANNER IN WHICH THIS GOLDEN LIQUID IS MADE, is when the distillation process is taking place – between November and the end of March the following year. It is still enigmatic to most outsiders, but to a distiller, the chemistry that takes place inside a traditional Charentais copper still is intuitive knowledge.

PP64/5: AN UNUSED STILL AT DELAMAIN HAS A WOOD-BURNING OVEN. IT IS KEPT IN IMMACULATE CONDITION AS A REMINDER OF OLD DISTILLATION METHODS.

During one of my visits to Frapin, one of the few family-owned cognac houses in the region, a couple of secrets were revealed. To stand in the pristine distillery is a memorable experience: the room is dominated by the four vast, gleaming copper stills built atop a red-brick square containing the fireplace. The cathedral-like space is clean, with nothing out of place. The cauldrons tower above any visitors, like copper gods awaiting their sacrificial litres of wine.

Even so, temperature and capacity gauges and other manmade machines allow the distiller to feel that he is in charge of the distillation process. In a small house such as Frapin's the distiller has to watch the four stills constantly when they are in operation, although in major houses such as Hennessy, Rémy Martin or Martell, it is not physically possible for one distiller to do this by himself.

Concentration on the task in hand is vital for success. This is the period when the art of distillation comes to the fore, when the company's future is truly in the hands (and mind) of a distiller.

As we have seen, the origins of the first cognac are lost back in the mists of time, and, despite an enormous amount of research undertaken by wine-writers and scholars, little can be stated as absolute truth. Scholars generally agree that the ancient Egyptians first discovered that the distillation of alcohol increased its strength as well as enhancing its flavours. This distilled alcohol probably would not have tasted like brandy; it was not based on grape wine, but on other fermented fruit spirits. However, it eventually led to the processes that would be applied to grape wine and result in the creation of the golden liquid that is cognac.

The origins of the word 'distillation' are Latin, from the verb *destillare*, meaning 'to drip' or 'to trickle down'. In basic terms, distillation reduces the amount of water in a fermented liquid, concentrating the alcohol. Wine contains both alcohol and water, but alcohol has a lower boiling point than water, and becomes vapour at 78.3°C (173°F). By collecting the vapour, the alcohol in wine can be separated from the water. This collected vapour, recondensed, has been called many names during its history, including 'the fiery soul of wine', the 'quintessence', the 'permanent water', 'fire water' and 'the water of life'. Each of these phrases imbue the spirit with great dignity.

In wine terms, the bridge between the ancient world and modern sciences was created by the Arabs, who passed their knowledge of distillation to Europeans when the former invaded Spain; it is quite possible, however, that travelling European scholars may have learned the principles of distillation from Arabic physicians as early as the 7th or 8th centuries. Our use of the Arabic words 'alcohol' and 'alembic' dates back to this very early period. However, more than one scholar has claimed that 12th century Christians at Salerno in Italy 'discovered' the distillation of alcohol from wine; this is still open to discussion (preferably over a bottle of cognac).

However, there is no doubt in any scholar's mind that, by the 13th century, the art of distilling spirit from wine as a raw material was widely practised throughout Europe – that is, in Ireland, Scotland, Spain and Germany, but not necessarily in France. There is no real evidence that the French carried out the distillation of any spirit until the 14th century. Cyril Ray, in his amusing and informative work *Cognac* (Peter Davies, 1973) writes this explanation:

'It may be they were happy enough with their wines, already of outstandingly high quality compared with those of other countries, until the Italians, from whom they learned much in the way of good living, taught them to drink, to enjoy and, in consequence, to make distilled and flavoured liqueurs.'

OPPOSITE: FEW WOOD-BURNING STILLS ARE IN USE NOW. THIS ONE, AT A E DOR, IS STOKED BY THE DISTILLER, CREATING A HUMID ATMOSPHERE IN THE DISTILLERY.

Eventually, the French found they were quite good at this process and now, some six centuries later, they distil some of the best *eaux-de-vie* in the world, including cognac.

THE PROCESS OF DISTILLATION

Alcohol, in its most common drinkable form, is the result of the fermentation of fruit – in the case of wine, of grapes. The alcoholic content of wine depends on the amount of fructose and other fruit sugars found in the grapes; the more of these sugars, the greater the resulting alcoholic strength. However, there is a limit to how strong wines can be, as fermentation stops once all sugars have been

used by yeasts, which are necessary for the fermentation, or once the strength is such that the yeasts stop their work. The maximum alcoholic strength of wine is 14 to 15 per cent alcohol by volume (abv), but most are well below this figure (fortified wines are stronger, but the increase in strength is due to the addition of brandy). Thus, the only way to increase the alcoholic content of any fully fermented wine is by distilling it.

Put simply, distillation is a process during which a liquid is heated so that it evaporates. As has been mentioned, the various constituents of wine evaporate at different temperatures. Since alcohol has a lower boiling point than water, it is given off as a vapour first; if this vapour is collected before the water boils, then alcohol can be separated from it, thus concentrating and increasing its strength. It is this process that is the key to making any brandy, including the finest cognacs.

Cognac is made from the wine of white grapes, which are mainly (95 per cent) Ugni Blanc and are harvested during October and November. The grapes are pressed without any delay, either by traditional horizontal plate presses or in more modern pneumatic presses. The juice is immediately run into stone, concrete or metal vats to start the fermentation process.

These stages are kept as pure as possible. The process known as *chaptalization* in which sugar is added during winemaking is forbidden in cognac production (although, as we shall see, sugar syrup can be added at the blending stage). Unlike still-wine production, no sulphur dioxide is used in the purification, or fining processes, either, as this could taint the subtle flavour of the finished cognac. After all, distillation concentrates the defects as well as the superb qualities of a wine, as any experienced distiller will tell you.

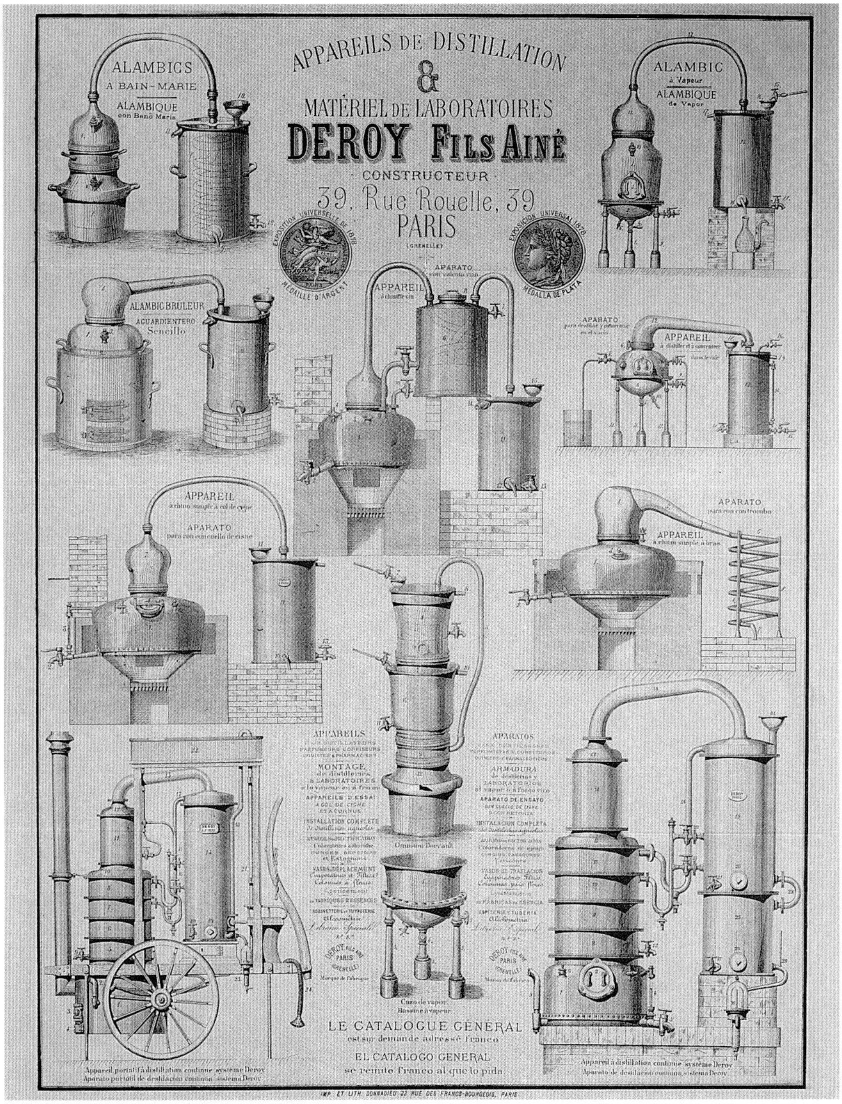

ABOVE: A GRAPHIC ADVERTISEMENT DATING FROM THE 1890S SHOWS THE VARIOUS PIECES OF APPARATUS USED TO MAKE AN ALEMBIC STILL.

After three weeks of fermentation, the process is halted. At this stage, the wine is only about eight to nine per cent alcohol – perfect for producing cognac; indeed, a stronger wine would produce an inferior brandy. The wine is also harsh and has a high acidity, making it unsuitable for consumption as a table wine.

Fuller-flavoured wine, made from more strongly flavoured grapes, would give the brandy too distinctive a flavour. The positive aspect of the Ugni Blanc grape is that it is neutral and does not overburden a wine with its own flavours, but still has enough created by the environment in which is grown (*see* Chapter 2) to influence the quality of the final cognac. This is the reason that, often, bad years for winemaking – when the wines are acidic (as in 1963,1968, 1972 and 1979, for example) – are good years for cognacs. Acidity gives a cognac its finesse.

Once fermented, the wine is not allowed to mature but is distilled immediately. The process begins only a month after the grapes have been harvested, and the entire operation is over by March 31st, because the age of a cognac is charted from April 1st. This type of dating is related to cash flow: if the spirit is not ready by the official date, then it is not officially a year old until the *following* March 31st.

The speed at which the wine is distilled enables the spirit to retain its freshness and original characteristics based on the soil and climate of the area, which are passed on by distillation to the finished cognac. For this reason, some houses have a vine-to-vat system of just two hours. As mentioned earlier, if the wine is not good, then its bad elements will be concentrated during distillation, and the resulting *eau-de-vie* will be bad as well. It takes about nine litres of wine to make just one bottle of cognac, so you can imagine how many tonnes of grapes it takes to make the wine to distil the *eau-de-vie*.

The skill of the distiller is to control the strength and quality of the alcohol as it leaves the still so that he is able to reduce the amount of unwanted impurities while retaining others that give the cognac its character. In order to get the right degree of alcohol (up to 72 per cent abv in cognac) the wine needs to be distilled twice. The first distillation, known as the *première chauffe*, produces 28 to 32 per cent abv, while the second takes it up to the required 72 per cent – although, as we shall see, there are proportions of the second distillate that are both stronger and weaker than this. It takes up to eight uninterrupted hours for the first three stages of the first distillation to be completed.

The distillation of cognac must, by law, take place in a copper still, the traditional Charentais *alambic à repasse*, that has hardly altered since the Dutch first developed it in the 17th century. Copper is important for many reasons: it not only helps spread the heat evenly, but it also helps retain the various fatty acids and any sulphur impurities in the wine, rather than releasing them into the vapour. In addition, copper is a neutral metal and does not react with heated wine. This *alambic à repasse* is shaped like an onion (the *cucurbite*) with a smaller vessel, the *chapiteau*, on top of it.

One of the modern refinements used by today's distiller is a pre-heater (*chauffe vin*), situated before the main heated vessel. This preheats the wine, cutting down the amount of heat required and the time taken to start the evaporation process. Tiffon, one of the older private houses located in Jarnac, uses a preheater as part of its production process. Not all producers, however, are happy with this money-saving technique, and some avoid using it in case it oxidizes the wine.

Another refinement is the use of the swan-neck tube, or *col de cygne*, which generally replaced a larger head and more angular tube known as the Moor's

C7
CT 28
CC 25

head, or *tête de maure*. The latter did not remove as many impurities, which yielded a less-smooth cognac than the swan-neck does.

When wine is fermented, a sort of 'sludge' accumulates in the bottom of the fermentation tank. This is known as the lees (*lie* in French), and consists mainly of dead yeast cells. Yeasts – whether natural or introduced – are what transform fruit sugars in the grapes into alcohol. During distillation, the wine, usually with its lees, is pumped from its fermentation vat into a lower vessel (the boiler), underneath which a flame is lit. By law, the heat is applied in the form of a flame to the outside of the still (as opposed to using heating coils inside it).

Originally this was provided by a wood or coal fire, but now natural gas is more commonly used, making it easier to supply and control the necessary steady stream of heat. The temperature and speed of heating are carefully controlled. As the wine is heated, the alcohol, along with its impurities and congeners, is given off as a vapour when the temperature reaches 78.3°C (173°F), leaving the majority of water behind in the still. These vapours are trapped in the *chapiteau* at the top of the still, then led via the *col de cygne* into a coiled tube (the *serpentin*) situated in a cooling tank, where the vapour is cooled so that it condenses into a liquid once again. This liquid, known as the *broullis*, is then collected. The *brouillis* is only 27 to 30 per cent alcohol and slightly cloudy.

PP74/75: A MODERN DISTILLERY GLEAMS WITH THE REFLECTION OF BRIGHT COPPER STILLS BRIMMING WITH THE LIQUID THAT WILL BECOME COGNAC.

It is at this stage that the distiller's unique art comes into its own. As the vapours are condensed, they are split into three distinct sections. The separation of these is known as *la coupe* – 'the cut' – and requires great skill. The first part of the *brouillis* to condense what is called the *têtes*, 'heads', (about 1.2 per cent of the distillate), which will be put into the next new wine and will therefore be distilled twice again. The second part is *la coeur*, the heart, which is colourless and almost without aroma or taste; this is the raw cognac, which legally can be up to, but no more than, 72 per cent alcohol.

Once the percentage of alcohol drops to 60 per cent, the third portion called the *queues*, 'tails', appears and is separated; later it is put into the next *brouillis*, and will be distilled just once more. These 'tails' are much lower in alcohol and carry impurities as well as some desirable flavour characteristics. Recycling the tails affects the final flavour of the cognac, making it more fruity.

The point at which the *queues* are separated makes a lot of difference to the final brandy, in terms of both strength and flavour. The more *queues* that are allowed to remain in the *coeur*, the lower the brandy's alcoholic strength and the richer the flavour. However, as well as increasing the number of welcome flavours, the tails can also increase the number of undesirable impurities, so great skill is required to know exactly when to cut them off.

The *brouillis* is undrinkable and is returned to the cleaned still (*chaudière*) for a second distillation: *la bonne chauffe*. This distillation takes longer, perhaps up to 12 hours, and there are heads and tails as in the first distillation. These are put aside as before, to be distilled with the next *brouillis*. The trick is to capture the wine's bouquet before it wafts away.

With both stages, great care is taken. The spirit is tasted and tested constantly, and the alcohol meter is watched so that, at the right moment, the heads and tails can be separated most effectively. All of this activity is carried out in a 24-hour period. It is not unusual for the distiller and the team will sleep in the distillery 'just in case'.

It is this second distillation that gives cognac many of its characteristics. Other brandies, such as armagnac, are distilled only once. For cognac, there are strict regulations regarding the second distillation. The still must not have a capacity greater than 30 hectolitres (hl), and the amount of *broullis* must not exceed 25 hl (about 3,000 bottles) at a time. The reason for this is because if a bigger vessel were used (and the temptation is there to use bigger vessels to cut time and costs), certain qualities of the final product would be lost.

THE IMPORTANCE OF THE LEES

As explained earlier in this chapter, it is the distiller's art and experience that give each cognac house its unique flavour. For smaller, traditional houses such as Frapin, which produces only Grande Champagne cognacs (under the guidance of distiller Roger Livet and *maître de chai* Olivier Paultes) and the house of Pierre Ferrand (where Patrick Guidicelli is in charge of distilling), the individual characteristics of their cognacs are also due, in part, to the fact that the base wines are distilled together with their lees. Even a large house such as Rémy Martin, under the guardianship of its *maître de chai*, Georges Clot, distills on the lees (*sur lie* in French) during the manufacturing process because he feels it provides their cognacs with a signature flavour.

When a wine is distilled on the lees, it is harder to distil, but the procedure produces a more complex cognac, with more body, more power and longer-lasting flavour. For the distiller and his team in a smaller house, distilling on the lees is relatively easy, since perhaps only four stills must be monitored. However, for distillers in the larger houses, which own 20 or more stills, it is a more difficult prospect.

Yet lees give complexity to a cognac by reacting when water is added to it. Even so, many distillers prefer to avoid distilling the lees because it eases the distillation. There is also an underlying concern among many houses that the heated residue from the lees might produce a burnt flavour in the cognac. This is where the distiller's experience comes in.

Regardless of the risks involved, Frapin distils *sur lie*. So does Rèmy Martin, and you can can smell it and taste it in the company's cognacs.

'I will show you a little secret,' Frapin's Olivier Paultes explained to me. 'If you take an *eau-de-vie* and put a little water into it, you will know if the wine has been distilled with the lees or not. Within five minutes you will see a little blue haze in the liquid; this hint of blue comes from the lees.

'When you taste a cognac distilled without the lees,' he continued, 'its flavour stops quickly in the mouth, and you sip it again for more of the taste. When a cognac from Grande Champagne grapes is distilled on its lees, the taste is very long and the fruity aromas stay in the mouth.'

In a small cupboard in Frapin's tasting room is a collection of badly distilled *eaux-de-vie* that had been put in a cask and aged. Olivier Paultes uses these rejected samples, collected over the years from the Bureau National Interprofessionel du Cognac's laboratory, to show the difference between the good, the bad and the best. He gave me a small tasting glass of one such incorrectly distilled *eau-de-vie*, and immediately I could sense its strongly metallic nose and its coppery taste. If you put a bad *eau-de-vie* in cask and age it, its bad qualities will not disappear, even with skilful blending. This example is a reminder of the importance of the distillation process and the skill of the distiller.

THE AGEING PROCESS BEGINS

The distiller's work is only one stage of the journey from grape to fine cognac. The next is to age the cognac, to 'rest it' in an oak cask, where it will gain all the colour, flavour and finesse required for it to become greatly admired when it is finally put into the bottle.

The pale, clear liquid that is freshly distilled *eau-de-vie* is a rough, neutral spirit that bears little resemblance to a smooth, fine cognac. It must now be placed in oak for a period lasting from a few years to possibly 50 to 60; however, three years' barrel-age is the legal minimum for any cognac, and VSOP (Very Special Old Pale) cognacs boast a minimum of five. Even if a blended cognac contains extremely old *eau-de-vie*, the cognac houses are not allowed to put any age over seven years on their labels, due to difficulties in quality control.

OPPOSITE: FIRING THE BARRELS IS AN ESSENTIAL PART OF THE SEASONING PROCESS FOR NEW OAK.

The decision of which *eau-de-vie* to age is made by the *maître de chai* and his team of blenders. After the March 31st deadline, distillers send samples of *eaux-de-vie* from the second distillation to selected houses for tasting. Here, the samples are checked rigorously; notes are made of the colour, flavour, and any other characteristics deemed important in producing the final cognac. Some of the older houses have important indexed notes of *eau-de-vie* years and their unique characteristics dating back for almost a century. When the *maître de chai* has made his selection from the samples presented to him, the immature stocks are put into casks, where the mysterious alchemy of the ageing process begins.

Some cognacs are grown, fermented, distilled, aged and blended at the same vineyard, for instance as at Frapin. When this occurs, you can be assured the

product is of the highest quality. Small growers distil for their own use, too. They may keep a cognac for, say, 40 or 50 years, and when they want to realize its cash value (perhaps when a daughter is to be married or it is a special anniversary), they approach one of the established, quality houses and sell it to them for the right price. And the houses are willing to pay well for cognac aged skilfully in the right conditions.

In fact, many larger houses do not grow their own grapes, nor do they distill at all. What they do is buy distilled *eau-de-vie* and mature it in casks in their own cellars, then blend it for bottling and shipping to countries throughout the world. Some of the families who grow and distil wines for the established houses, including Hennessy, Courvoisier, Delamain, Hine and Martell, have been doing so for generations and have learned the way these houses prefer their *eaux de vie* – instinctively, they produce them, as it were, to order.

THE ART OF THE CASKS

Let me explain what I have learnt about the making of the casks, the steps of the ageing process and blending. Casks are made from open-grained French oak harvested from the ancient Limousin or the newer Tronçais forests which lie to the north of Cognac. The use of oak from these particular areas is by custom rather than by regulation (although it is laid down in the regulations that oak is to be used and it must be at least 50 years old). Oak casks from other countries such as America and Russia are available, but each is quite different from the other, both in colour and texture.

The quality of the oak is very important, as it is the chemicals in the oak – the tannins and lignins – and their interaction with the maturing spirit that give cognac both its colours and flavours. The style of the cognac houses is, in essence, defined by the qualities of the wood in which their cognacs are kept.

When it finishes its second distillation, cognac is colourless; it is the tannin in the oak casks that imparts that glorious, golden colour. At first, the tannins also add a bitter taste to the immature spirit, but this mellows with time. The lignins – the substances which make oak cells rigid and woody – contribute to the flavours of the cognac. The oak is also porous, which allows the cognac to make a limited contact with the surrounding air; oxygen mellows the rawness of the distilled *eau-de-vie* as well as causing some of it to evaporate.

Limousin oak is tough wood and has a fatter, looser grain than that of the Tronçais oak; thus, it lets in more oxygen as well as allowing more of its fine tannin into the spirit, making it more useful for cognacs requiring a long maturation. These heavy Limousin trunks, some up to 100 years old, used to be floated down the River Charente in cognac's early years. This was both speedy and economical, since the Limousin forests were not far away in the hills to the east of nearby Angoulême.

The closer-grained Tronçais oak comes from forests planted to grow oak for France's navy in the 1750s. These are located further afield, near Burgundy country. Tronçais wood does not release so many tannins, and contains more lignins, making it a better wood for cognacs that do not require long ageing. Interestingly, most of the houses I visited were adamant that they would use only Limousin for their cognacs. Some, however, use both.

Cask-making is a traditional business of the region and many of the larger cognac houses have their own cooperages. Altogether there are over 500 coopers employed in the area, just to service the cognac industry. The casks vary in size from 270 to 450 litres each. In general terms, the smaller the cask, the more wood you will taste in the cognac. Currently, the 350-litre cask is the most popular size, providing the right balance to produce the best-quality cognac.

Cognac casks are unique in many ways. The oak has to be at least 50 years old, and only the trunk from the roots to the lower branches can be used. This is the section with the least knots and other undesirable faults.

Once the pre-sliced trunks reach the *tonnellerie* (cooperage), they are left outside in stacks, letting the air dry them naturally. The drying rate is about one year for every centimetre of thickness and, as each plank measures about six centimetres thick, the process takes about six years per plank. During this time, the more bitter aspects of the tannins disappear and a mould develops, which works on the lignins in the wood. The lignin then takes on a vanilla flavour that is dissolved by the acid and alcohol in the cognac when it is poured into the cask, and this is responsible for the hint of vanilla in the final spirit.

Cask-construction follows a traditional method. The wood is sliced along the grain, not sawn across. Great care is taken by the cooper, and casks can reveal the idiosyncrasies of the men who made them, like signatures to a work of art. One mistake in construction can have dire consequences for the taste of a cognac: a leak means both the producer (and those notorious angels) lose more, and a loose stave can add a disquieting taste to a cognac.

Traditionally, the hoops that stretch around the staves were made of strips of chestnut or even oak, and were concentrated at either end of the cask, which made it easy to roll the cask on the quayside and in the cellar. Today, however, most are bound with metal hoops – and they are still easy to roll. The casks are made using neither glue or nails so that the flavour is not altered in any unnatural way.

SEASONING AND CELLARING

New casks are seasoned with lesser-quality cognac and are not used for better grades until the wood has mellowed, and the brandy has reduced the rawness of the tannin. In general terms, if better-quality spirit is stored in new barrels, it is only for between six months and a year. It is then moved on to older, seasoned barrels.

Young cognac is stored in new oak casks for up to six months. The cognac is then tasted and moved to older casks, where it will stay the *maître de chais* decides to move it into either a demi-john or a bottle. Frapin uses what it calls a 'red' cask for five years, and then takes the cognac out of the red and moves it into old wood: 'wood that is very old with the flavours of past cognacs'. 'These casks give a very good aroma,' Paultes explained.

By law, the cognac must be aged for at least 30 months. However, 40 – or in some cases, 50 – years is considered the longest a cognac should remain in cask, since by then it will have reached its peak. If the cognac is kept longer than this, it is moved into large, 25-litre glass jars – *bonbonne*, or demijohns – which are airtight and prevent any further maturation. It's like being 40 forever.

The casks are stored in cellars known as *chais* (cellars), which are used exclusively for cognac. The atmosphere in these *chais* is extremely important as it is the balance between humidity and dryness that controls the evaporation from the oak casks. A dry cellar evaporates water and alcohol and gives more finesse to the cognac; a wet cellar evaporates alcohol only and gives a rounder taste to the final product. The oldest prized cognacs are stored in a darkened cellar known as *le paradis*, away from the other cellars. These are usually stored for the next generation, or for the family's own use.

One of my favourite places is Hine's *chai*, located on the cobbled quay at Jarnac, where the stone floors are covered with white gravel chips . 'The gravel is used to absorb the humidity of the ground and release it into the air,' says Bernard Hine. 'Humidity regulation is important to provide a regular ageing to cognac and give it a mellow, smooth aroma.'

Consequently, on my many visits to other cellars in Cognac I immediately checked the ground's surface. Where the cellars were enormous and multi-levelled, the chalky addition was not always necessary. In some cellars, the casks are moved around from dry cellars – generally those directly under the roof – to wet cellars underground, usually with water seeping through the mould-encrusted stone walls.

Rémy Martin built 26 vast cellars at Merpins, a little way out of Cognac's town centre, in 1966, after the mayor of the time voiced concern about the risk of fire from all that alcohol in one place. At Rémy, *maître de chai* Georges Clot decides which blend and cask goes in which *chai*, because each has its own humidity, temperature and history. On one of my visits he took me to the smallest of the cellars, a stone structure with steps leading to large, wooden doors studded with black mould. Even the stone balusters have moss growing through the mould. A small key unlocked the 'gateway to paradise', for within lay the family's reserve collection, locked away yet again down on the lowest level, behind iron bars. The cellar has the atmosphere of a dank dungeon, but it is one in which I would happily be chained.

Monsieur Clot led me through the first level, filled with casks. 'This is young Louis XIII,' he said, gesturing at the large area on the ground-floor level. We moved down to the next level, where he took the bung out of a cask, plunged the long glass pipette – a glass tube with a suction action – into it, and drew out a small amount of cognac. He poured it into a tasting glass (which he must carry in a secret pocket in his overcoat, for I did not see him pick it up on the way in!) and offered me a sip.

'I finished this blend last year, and it will be released in 2003 as Louis XIII,' he offered as an explanation of his generosity. We swirled, held it up to the light (all the lights have black, metal covers with the Rémy Martin logo stamped in them, so the 'Rémy light' is always shining on the future cognac) and then we sipped. It was powerful, rich and almost ready.

The bung replaced, we moved down one more level, underground. Here, sat older casks, drained of all their tannin, still with the chestnut strips around them. Around 100 years ago, they would have been carried by horse and cart; now they are filled with 50-year-old cognac, I expect. Monsieur Clot wandered off to a dark corner and gestured for me to follow. I stepped through some iron gates and sniffed the damp air. Seven barrels of unparalleled, extravagant cognac – 1952 Grande Champagne laid down by Dominique Hériard-Dubreuil's grandfather, André Renaud – were in front of me. We went through the same process of slipping in the pipette, swirling and sipping, but this was an entirely different taste – an exceptional flavour of fruit, a full body, richness and a superb softness. These casks are for the family's use only, and I am grateful that I had the opportunity to sip such a sublime liquid. It was a taste that will remain in my memory for many years.

We locked the gates and walked up through the levels, surrounded by history, conscious of the mushroom fragrance one can find only in a *chai*, turning off each light as we went. At the imposing front door, Monsieur Clot explained that

the electricity in the whole complex is turned off each night as a safety precaution, leaving only the angels to watch over the treasure.

Earlier that same week, I had learned a fascinating ecological fact while exploring the dark cellar at Frapin with Paultes. Here, thick cobwebs trail down from centuries-old beams and also cover the casks. Cobwebs are common in cellars, but I hadn't realized the reason for so many of them until Paultes explained, as he led me through the dusty ancient casks lined up in the cellar, that the spiders which crawl all over the *chai* are useful, eating little bugs that live on the oak and chestnut hoops wrapped around the cask, thus preserving the integrity of both wood and wine.

THE EFFECTS OF AGE

While the cognac is resting, cellar-masters such as Clot and Paultes continually taste and move the casks to ensure that the final quality is the way they want it to be. Usually the position of cellar-master is held by a man. I know of only a few female blenders, one of whom is Madame Betty Lesueur, the distiller at Hennessy's Camp Romain.

PP88/9: THE SKILLED PROCESS AT THE TONNELLERIE IS LITTLE CHANGED FROM ITS EARLY TRADITIONS. THE PREFERRED OAK IS FROM LIMOUSIN FORESTS.

The moment cognac is put into the older casks (which have already given out most of their tannin), the ageing process will slow down; the cognac will gradually gain its roundness and mellow taste, as well as a more complex bouquet. It will acquire first the vanilla, floral and honey aromas; the leather and tobacco come later. The liquid will finally take on a sylvan, fungal flavour as well as the celebrated *rancio* that characterizes aged cognacs. As the years pass, alcohol and a percentage of the volume decrease through evaporation from the casks. As mentioned previously, this loss is known as the *part des anges* or 'angels' share'. The angels in the region must be very thirsty as, amazingly, the loss through evaporation amounts to over 20 million bottles a year; looked at another way, however, this is only three to six per cent of cognac's volume. The reduction in alcoholic strength is even less, working out at 0.4 to 0.5 per cent. Once a year, the loss from a cask is made up by topping it up with newer cognac or, in the case of unblended cognacs, from spirit of the same age.

The familiar tiny fungus, *Torula compniacencis richon*, also feeds on the vapours resulting from the evaporation, which is why a black mould covers the roofs of the cellars and surrounding buildings. One of the cellar-masters told me an amusing tale concerning the Bureau National Interprofessionnel du Cognac. Back in 1950, when it was time to check on who declared their cognac stocks for tax and who didn't, the controllers hired an aircraft and flew low across all six *crus* – even lower above private houses or warehouses that were more than usually covered with the black fungus (a sign that cognac was being stored in the attic) and not on their list of declared cognac stocks!

THE BLENDER'S ART

While ageing is going on, and again after it has finished, the subtle art of the blender comes into play. He takes cognacs of varying ages and from different vineyards and marries them to produce the flavour, colour and scent of the house. Max Cointreau is one of cognac's revered 'noses', a former mayor of Cognac and a major player in the development of the cognac business.

According to Max, blenders literally 'bring up' the cognacs: '[The blender] has journeyed many, many years preparing the cognacs for bottling,' he says.

'It is a difficult job, because you have to imagine how it will look, this *eau-de-vie* being blended with that *eau-de-vie*, for the 20- to 25-year period it will be in the cask.'

The most important tool a blender has to enable him to do his job is his nose. His taste-buds are also important, but secondary. Blending is a human skill, and the blender relies completely on his nose and palate. The creative skill of blender is to come up with various flavours that work together without dominating or contradicting each other. It is like creating a cocktail, balancing earthiness, fruitiness, flowery aromas, sweetness, spiciness and *rancio*.

From the start of a blend, there about about nine stages occur to produce the final cognac. The contents of each cask are sampled periodically and detailed notes are made in the *maître de chai's* cellar book. He also is in cgarge of looking after the ageing stock in the cellars.

OPPOSITE: ATMOSPHERIC CONDITIONS ARE MONITORED IN THE AGEING VAULT AT CAMUS. THESE CASKS HOLD COGNAC NEAR THE END OF ITS MATURATION.

First, a blender will decide which of the six main *crus* he wants to use. The origin of the wine is important, as some of the lesser cognacs will never improve beyond certain point however long they are kept. Each *cru* has a special characteristic; for instance, Fins Bois cognacs are floral, and this character will come through in the final blend.

A blend of VS can be made of up to 40 *eaux-de-vie* from all six *crus*; Rémy Martin's Cordon Bleu is a combination of up to 200 cognacs. A blend of VSOP may contain up to 60 cognacs from all six regions. An XO might contain up to 80 different *eaux-de-vie*. And of course, the style of the final cognac varies from house to house. There is no precise indication on a bottle as to how long the cognac has been matured or where it has come from (unless it is

Grande Champagne, or Fine Champagne). As a guide, VS or (Three Star) has usually been matured for three to five years. VSOP (Very Special [or Superior] Old Pale) is between five and 10 years old, sometimes 12 years old. Napoléon is usually between seven and 15 years old, while XO is above 20 years old, usually 25 to 35 years old.

These and other names are all rather vague and are but a rough guide to maturity. However, any such name should refer to the *youngest* spirit in the blend and give some idea of the minimum age of the cognac.

A later batch of, say, an XO must be identical in colour and flavour to the same product made for the past 10 or 20 years. This explains why the larger houses hold so much stocks of a particular cognac. When they want to recreate it, a change may have occurred in the cask. However slight this may be, it is immediately apparent to a blender and he must find a way to counteract it.

Just as with the recent spate of cigar blends, the challenge for today's master-blender is in creating new styles. There is also the new trend for cognac that is suitable for use as a mixer, such as Hennessy's Pure White, Rémy Martin's Rémy Red and Rémy Silver (blended with vodka), and Camus' label, Neon.

Another role of the blender is to finish the cognac. The alcoholic strength has been reduced from the 72 per cent at distillation, by loss of alcohol through evaporation, but it is still too strong for the market and must be reduced to about 40 per cent abv by the addition of distilled water or *petits eaux* (low-strength brandy). This is done over a period of time to allow it to blend evenly, and should be carried out at least six months before bottling. Some cognacs from smaller select houses are sold at over 40 per cent abv; this is shown on the label.

In order to obtain consistent colour (or a darker colour that some markets prefer), some producers add caramel in small quantities to their cognacs. This does not alter the spirit's taste, but it does produce a consistently rich, golden colour. Another additive in the blender's palette (usually introduced at the same time) is sugar syrup, which is added to get a sweeter, rounder flavour that some producers want, particularly for the younger, less-mellowed brandies. Yet another way of affecting the final taste is by introducing oak chips *(boisé)* soaked in an older cognac into the barrels, possibly for several years, in order to promote the premature ageing of some younger cognacs.

There was a move by some of the big houses at the end of the 20th century to produce cognac from single distilleries or from single districts, in order to expand their market share. This was the result of a reaction to what had become a difficult period for them as some previously buoyant markets had slumped. Whether this situation will continue remains to be seen in the future.

Unblended cognacs are also produced from a single year (vintage). This trend, to some extent, is pushing the responsibility for a cognac's characteristics away from the blender and back to the distiller.

The temperatures, the moment the 'tail' is cut off and whether, during the initial fermentation, the wine should still contain the lees all becomes much more important than with multiple-blended cognacs, whose heritage stretches back over the past three centuries.

Despite technological advances and modern distilling methods, the process has changed little from the 1800s, when the founders of today's cognac houses built their wood-burning distilleries throughout the region. Theirs was a harder task, but one they faced with integrity and determination.

COGNAC'S THERAPEUTIC QUALITIES

An urban legend has it that no one who lives in Jarnac or Cognac ever has a cold or influenza. Not having seen doctors' medical records, I cannot possibly comment. However, thanks to its alcohol content, cognac has medical virtues.

Through its ageing process cognac undergoes physiological reactions, with an increase in acids and aldehydes (non-alcohol elements). The resultant alcohol is stimulating and regulating to the heart. Because it is usually drunk after a meal, mixing it with food, it does not create that nagging feeling of hunger often generated by pre-dinner cocktails. It provides a feeling of comfort while helping the digestive process by raising gastric secretions.

In his *L'Histoire du Cognac* (Stock, 1935) Robert Delamain states that: 'Its diuretic and tonic action is especially strong and much higher than in neutral alcohol. Which is why it is so efficient in illnesses that generate fever, influenza, pneumonia and typhoid fever.' His research concluded that the men working in the damp cognac-soaked atmosphere of the storehouse rarely caught tuberculosis.

OPPOSITE: A CASK OF 1965 IS SAMPLED AS PART OF THE CONTINUAL MONITORING OF QUALITY AS THE COGNAC MATURES. PP98/9: INTENSE CONCENTRATION IS REQUIRED BY THE COOPER – THEIR SKILL IS DEVELOPED OVER YEARS.

During prohibition cognac was the only spirit allowed into the United States, purportedly for 'medicinal reasons'. It would be beneficial to explore its curative capabilities created by its nature, its origin and ageing process.

In the meantime, a sip or two after-dinner has become my antidote to winter chills. If you live in an inclement climate, you may well wish to do the same. Salut!

1965

FAMILY, HERITAGE & INFLUENCE

'When my mother brought in the fruit salad she brought the dish with a bottle cognac and my father would add the cognac – whoosh!'

CHARLES BRAASTAD-DELAMAIN

IN SOME FAR-FLUNG FOREIGN COURTYARD IS A PIECE OF LAND THAT WILL REMAIN FOREVER ENGLAND. Here, behind the typically French façade of Martell's head office, is the Founder's House, the small home that Jersey-born merchant Jean Martell built when he first settled in Cognac in 1715. Because I make no claim to having an historian's perspective, I prefer to present a snapshot of the way life might have been during this period, based on my own visit and observations there.

PP100/1: THE 1987 COLBERT TROPHY AWARDED ANNUALLY BY RÉMY MARTIN TO YOUNG SCULPTORS.

As I wandered through Jean Martell's stone house, I saw where he would have sat to write his stock orders, spoken to the cellar master, and ordered goods and chattels from suppliers back home. Glancing at the cupboards full of his large, neatly detailed accounts ledgers, I began to put together a vision of the man who played one of the most important roles in this century's development of cognac as a world-renowned spirit. He was even more admirable because he was, as acquaintances at the time observed, less ambitious to do things on a large scale than to do them little and well.

The front door of Martell's Founder's House was of heavy oak, the ceilings criss-crossed with dark, timber beams. The floors were stone, the walls timber-panelled and unpainted. The pieces of furniture showed that their owner was ever the man of high fashion, for they were unique, made especially for someone who knew exactly what he wanted. Martell's Jamaican mahogany desk, dating from around the 1730s, was a fine piece, made ostensibly for writing, yet in a moment the top could be turned into a table for playing cards. As a Cognaçais had earlier remarked to me, *sotto voce*, 'They were all gamblers, the merchants of Cognac. Great gamblers.'

Letters of credit, letters of introduction, bills of lading covered the top of this small but elegant desk. A literate man, Martell could read French and English, and regularly ordered books from a Monsieur Mesurier in Paris. Business books, one on the art of negotiation, still sat among his shelves. Many of his early dealings were with the Dutch East India Trading Company, and many of the items in his house reflected their origins. An 18th-century brass travelling compass and sextant was constantly in sight: a reminder of his father's travels as well as his own voyages abroad.

Like many a shrewd businessmen, Martell had irons in as many fires as possible. The trade in *eaux-de-vie* was buoyant in the 18th century, but it didn't hurt to trade in other desirable things. Diversity in commodities supported and helped to build his cognac business, always cash-demanding. A shipment of *eau-de-vie* arrived in London, where the ship was then loaded with coal, wool, linen, wheat and even cane-hooped petticoats. In one letter from his archives, Martell wrote to his mother asking her to send him samples of men's stockings. His own, worn in Cognac after a trip to London, had been admired tremendously by those he had met en route, and he could see a profit in them.

While *eaux-de-vie* and other goods were sent to the Dutch East India Company, tea, coffee and cocoa beans and tobacco returned on the same ships.

From Holland, for forward shipment to far-away exotic ports, came silk, folding travelling lamps, shirt cloth and beer. And tulip bulbs. A man had to exercise caution when dealing in tulip bulbs, for they were expensive commodities during the early 1700s and many a wealthy entrepreneur had kissed his fortune goodbye speculating on the value of such delicate plants.

Martell, however, was shrewd in business. He was also a good shot, frequently joining shoots around the countryside with other leading merchants, bagging birds for supper to have with bread (from the grain he imported), local and imported cheese, and beer. He was a man who missed nothing. He even liked to be on the quayside when his stocks were being loaded, revelling in the atmosphere of men shouting orders across the gangplank in different languages (Dutch, Norwegian, English and French) as they supervised the loading, listening for the clip-clop of horses hooves clattering across the cobblestones, pulling Martell carts that carried only a limited number of 34-hectolitre casks (the size of each cask was exactly the same width as the cart).

Jean Martell was almost a modern man in his approach to business, not only in his habit of reading of books on negotiating skills, but also in his constant monitoring of exchange rates. Like others in the cognac trading business at this time, he also did as much as he could to guarantee a good price for his stocks of *eaux-de-vie*. He bought well, kept them in storage, waited for an opportune moment, then sold them to the market with a favourable profit. In a letter to a friend, a Mr Kastell, dated May 14, 1721, he wrote: 'I can say without boasting that I have one of the best businesses in the region...'.

Not bad for the son of a Jersey merchant and navigator. The Martell family had lived on the Channel island since the 13th century. Jean was born in 1694, in the parish of St Brelades, the son of Thomas and Marthe Hérault, the second of eight children. His father died when he was only five years old, but he nonetheless played an important role in young Jean's early development, firing the young boy's imagination and spirit of adventure.

After working as a merchant for seven years on neighbouring Guernsey, Jean Martell headed for France, settling in Cognac when he saw the potential of the region's already celebrated *eau-de-vie*. Initially, he shipped products back to Guernsey and Jersey, traditional clearing houses for goods later smuggled into England (by the end of the 18th century, smugglers had become the biggest importers of French goods into the island). Shipments to Holland and the great Hanseatic ports of Hamburg and Lubeck followed.

His first marriage, in 1726 at the age of 32, was to Jeanne Brunet, daughter of a cognac merchant. It was this marriage that established Martell's roots firmly in Cognac. He was widowed early, not remarrying until 1737; this time, the bride was Rachel Lallemand, great-great-granddaughter of Jacques Roux, who had been selling *eau-de-vie* as early as 1610. When he died in 1753, Jean Martell was a major force in the development of cognac trading. He had begun life as a Protestant and ended as a Catholic, sensing it was the best way for his children to survive the 1685 revocation of the Edict of Nantes, which had forced Protestantism back underground.

If Martell is representative of the type of man who came to Cognac in search of liquid gold, then his marriage is representative of the kinds of opportunities that were on offer to help find it. The story of cognac is as much about the fairer sex and marriage as it is about religion and *eau-de-vie*. It was only natural that a new young man in town should present himself to one of the leading families and ask for a daughter's hand in marriage, particularly if the dowry was a cellar full of ageing *eau-de-vie*. Interestingly, though, the people of Cognac did not seem to mix with the families of Jarnac.

Examples of other advantageous marriages include Phillipe Augier, founder of the oldest cognac house (1643), who married the daughter of a wealthy banker and paper merchant from Angoulême. Sadly, this house and label no longer exists since Seagram bought it.

James Delamain married Marie Ranson, daughter of Isaac Ranson, one of the most respected men in the region at the time. The year before Martell established his company, Paul-Emile Rémy Martin had married Marie Geay.

The tradition of marrying into business seems to have run in some families. For example, the Irish Brigades officer, Richard Hennessy, who came from a Catholic family with a Cork heritage, settled in Cognac in 1765, after marrying first in Ostende. His wife gave birth to three sons – Jacques, Georges, and Richard. Augier became connected to the Martells through marriage, and one of the Martell family, Frédéric-Gabriel (born in 1745), later married Marie-Anne-Marthe Broussard de Fontmarais. In 1795 Jacques Hennessy married Marthe-Henriette Martell during the French Revolution, and their daughter, Lucie-Hélène Hennessy, born in 1796, married Jean Gabriel Martell (a Protestant) in 1816. Richard Hennessy died in 1800.

THE CENTURY OF EXPANSION

The 1700s were a period of economic expansion, and in France, cognac merchants were the driving force behind it. They had substantial incomes; they travelled and bought and sold the latest commodities that were in demand.

ABOVE: THOMAS HINE, THE YOUNG MAN FROM DORSET WHO ARRIVED IN JARNAC TO LEARN FRENCH, MARRIED WELL AND ENDED UP OWNING A COGNAC HOUSE.

From 1701 until 1714, the War of Spanish Succession disrupted trade with England and other parts of Europe. Added to this, a harsh frost wiped out most of the vineyards in the Saintogne province in 1709, and the vineyards had to be replanted. Brandy, however, was still getting through via the Channel Islands and other nefarious ways and there were still advertisements for 'Old Coniak Brandy' for 10 shillings a gallon in London newspapers around 1710 (the price was one shilling more than for brandy from other regions, but it was better quality). London merchant's stocks grew low until 1714, when the Peace of Utrecht between England, France and Holland signalled the reopening of trade.

Alphonse Prunier had established a cognac shipping business in 1700. (The company is now run by Susan Burnez, descendant of Jean Burnez, nephew of Alphonse Prunier.) Paul-Emile Rémy Martin, a Charentais winegrower, established his company in 1724, planting vineyards in the best regions of the Grande and Petite Champagne *crus*. He grew Colombard and Folle Blanche grapes, and used only Limousin oak casks to age his stocks. Martin was a perfectionist, aiming to produce the best cognac he could with what 'tools' he had available. The quality of his *eau-de-vie* so impressed the French king, Louis XV, that in spite of the 1731 royal decree forbidding anyone from planting new vineyards, Martin was granted a unique licence in 1738 to expand his vine holdings in Grande Champagne.

By 1726, the brandy produced in Cognac had gained a certain reputation. Historian and government official Jean Gervais sealed its reputation in his memorandum of 1726 on the export of *eaux-de-vie*. 'The Cognac brandy,' he wrote, 'is considered the best in the world.' Cognac, it seems, had become the standard against which all other brandies were to be measured.

SPIRIT OF SPECULATION

In 1730, cognac became the object of speculation. During the War of Spanish Succession, many grower-distillers had decided to store their best cognacs in cask until the end of the conflict, when trade, they hoped, would improve. Farmers who could not hold out until then sold their stocks for cash to merchants, who bought these stocks as a speculative venture. This state of affairs continued for the best part of 50 years, with *eau-de-vie* becoming a precious commodity whose price fluctuated according to the law of supply and demand (similar to the fervour over tulip bulbs in the Netherlands). Growers began to store *eau-de-vie* in order to sell it at the best price; since the quality of a vineyard's production was never the same from one year to another, and factoring in a few bad crops, they were fairly sure that the prices would rise.

It was noticed that, during the waiting period, *eau-de-vie* did not go bad; on the contrary, it got better every year, acquiring a more mellow taste, a deeper, more refined bouquet, and slowly gaining a range of flavours. It also slowly acquired a beautiful, warm shade of gold, which made it even more desirable. For this reason, merchants began to age *eau-de-vie* on purpose towards the end of the 18th century.

This, of course, resulted in a significant change in the way the spirit was sold. At the end of the 18th century, foreign buyers desired these aged qualities. Growers and farmers began to keep stocks at home. Wholesale traders – known as *négociants* – let stocks age in their casks, often on behalf of mainly English merchants. This also meant a change in the financial circumstances of some growers since their money was tied up for a longer period. The quality of oak used to make casks also became more important (*see* Chapter 3).

From this point on, *négociants* played a more important role in the production and development of cognac. Once the *eau-de-vie* had aged, the *négociant* took control. Some of these merchants worked for companies dating back to the 15th century, but up until the end of the 18th century, most *négociants* generally represented foreign buyers. Their growing influence was the result of new opportunities that arose when consumers started to appreciate aged *eau-de-vie*. The problem for farmers was that they had invested most of their assets in their property and lacked the working capital to keep *eau-de-vie* for long. So the *négociant* took on the role of banker or price-regulator in order to maintain a consistency of prices for foreign buyers, who could have become discouraged by the constant variations over the years.

The relationship between the *négociant* and his banker was as trusting as the relationship between the trade and the foreign buyer. *Négociants* recognized their responsibilities to the buyers, and in 1791, they signed a declaration stating the following:

> *'We, the undersigned, trading in eau-de-vie of cognac produced in the provinces of Saintogne and Angoumois, consider that the reputation of this eau-de-vie relies not only on its superior quality, but also on the fact that no foreign eau-de-vie is mixed with it. Therefore, anything that would compromise this trust would lower the demand, lower the prices and have grave consequences on what represents the major activity in this area.'*

This statement was intended to preserve the reputation of cognac against any unscrupulous activity. It was to be a long time before the special qualities of cognac were legally recognised by an international body – but this was a start on the road to self-protection.

FAMILIES & REVOLUTION

One of the major issues of the 18th century was taxation, which, throughout France, was growing extremely extortionate and complicated. For example, whenever a cask of brandy was shipped into Paris from the provinces, it gained domestic duties up to 10 times its value. In addition, the Cognaçais were paying double the taxes paid by merchants in La Rochelle. Despite various formal complaints from both peasant farmers and the aristocracy, nothing changed. This discontent grew during the subsequent decades and added to the discontent that would eventually evolve into the French Revolution of 1789.

Yet neither the tax system nor the threat of constant war deterred men from taking risks and starting up in the cognac trade. In 1762, James Delamain, from a Protestant Jarnac family, joined his father-in-law to establish Ranson and Delamain in Jarnac. Even during the Seven Years' War between England and France, which began in 1756, Delamain was selling cognac in Paris to the French army and navy stores.

The Delamain story begins in 1625, when Nicholas Delamain, a Huguenot born in Jarnac, travelled to London as a courtier to Princess Henrietta Maria of France, whereupon the princess married King Charles I of England and Ireland. Nicholas found England more hospitable to his religion than France, and he remained there, serving the English court well. In 1639, Delamain was given a knighthood and a small fortune, which he invested in properties in Ireland.

One of his descendants was a Dublin-based potter, Henry Delamain. His nephew was James, and it was he who returned to the family's birthplace, Jarnac, in 1759. In 1762, he married the daughter of Isaac Ranson, who had since 1725 been shipping wheat, wine and cognac to Ireland and Holland from Jarnac.

In 1797, Thomas Hine, a young Protestant from Dorset, married Françoise Elizabeth Delamain, James' daughter. Marrying a Delamain was considered a coup since, at this time, the Delamains were one of the most respected families in the business.

Thomas Hine was fortunate in his marriage in that it brought him respectability at the start. He had left the village of Beaminster in Dorset, England, in 1791 to travel to Cognac to learn French. He was 19 years old. Two years later, just as he about to return to his family, France declared war on England and he was imprisoned in the cells of the Château de Jarnac, where he met Richard Hennessy. This was during what the local people refer to as *La Grande Peur* – The Reign of Terror – and both Thomas Hine and Richard Hennessy were considered to be spies because they were English. James Delamain was in charge of the police in Jarnac and was therefore responsible for the two prisoners, who were better off than many, as they had money and could buy food. Delamain intervened and arranged for the young Englishmen's release, inviting Hine to his house, where Thomas met his wife-to-be, Françoise Elizabeth.

PP112/3: AN EVOCATIVE MOMENT AS STEAM DRIFTS THROUGH A VENT OUTSIDE COURVOISIER'S EUBERT DISTILLERY.

Hine went to work for Ranson and Delamain, and in 1817, he took over the company and changed its name to Thomas Hine & Co. Later that same year Hine cognac was shipped to England for the first time under the Hine name.

Hine's archives for the years between 1765 and the 1789 Revolution reveal an interesting correspondence between James Delamain and his bankers in Paris. The banker wrote to Mr Delamain, saying that he had received a request from a Mr Hennessy in Cognac for a certain amount of money. 'Do you think

I should lend it? Do you think it's safe?' Mr Delamain answered 'Yes, he's a very straight man, and honest. We have great confidence in him. He comes from a good Irish family...'. Today, Hine is owned by Hennessy, which in turn is owned by Louis Vuitton-Moët-Hennessy. Says Bernard Hine: 'It's fantastic! Now they are so big and we are so small. But in fact the green light – a recommendation to the bankers so that they would lend money to the Hennessys – was given by Delamain. It's good to find that letter after so many years.'

Baron Jean-Baptiste Antoine Otard and his friend Jean Dupuy had set up Cognac Otard in 1795, moving into the restored royal château (where François I was born) in 1796. During the Revolution, Otard was sentenced to death and was saved only by the intervention of friends. Otard had an important ally in Jean Dupuy's uncle, Léon, who had been selling cognac to the United States of America – at that time, a newly independent nation.

Martell had sent his first shipment to the States in 1784, followed later by Hennessy in 1794, who dealt with a Mr Jacob Schieffelin. The Schieffelin family remained Hennessy's agent in the United States for the next 200 years.

In 1804, Napoléon Bonaparte became Emperor of France, and war became a serious business for businesses, with the institution of the Continental Blockade in 1806. In theory, direct routes into England should have stopped altogether, but in fact, for a time, imports rose. After all, the English were not going to deprive themselves of a luxurious *digestif*.

During 1807, however, all French wines and spirits were banned from both the British Royal Navy and the Army, and this had a harmful effect on the cognac trade when combined with other trading bans. Consequently, the Cognaçais were relieved when Napoléon was finally defeated in 1815.

Béatrice Cointreau, chief executive of Frapin, told me that her young daughter was doing a project on the 'great Napoléon Bonaparte'. 'That man may have been good for the rest of France,' she sniffed, 'but he was bad – *very* bad – for Cognac!'

AN EXPLOSION OF COGNAC HOUSES

Napoléon's political downfall spawned a period of great activity in the towns of Cognac and Jarnac. The house of Croizet, based in Segonzac, was set up in 1805 by Léon Croizet, with vineyards in the heart of Grande Champagne; 1815 saw the start of Menard, also in the Grande Champagne area. Cognac Bisquit was set up in 1819 by 20-year-old Alexandre Bisquit, who was keen to exploit the removal of trade barriers after the fall of Napoléon. In 1820, Roullet and Co was formed, and in 1824, James's grandson, Henry Delamain, founded the house of Roullet and Delamain with his Roullet cousins.

OPPOSITE: THE INIMITABLE BERNARD HINE DOING WHAT HE DOES BEST – TASTING COGNAC.

In 1828, the house of Planat was established. Its founder was Olivier Planat, but it was his son, Oscar, a politician and a man of letters, who built up the prestigious company, not just by sales of his brand but also by supplying other major houses with *espirit de cognac* needed to improve their own blends.

Planat became wealthy and influential at government level – fortunately, not in a self-serving way. He worked to improve the public services in the town, producing plans for railways and canals, and increased the power of the prefecture and the civil tribune of Cognac. Elected mayor in 1878, Planat created a new town hall and park in the centre of the town. In return for his services, he was awarded the Croix de la Legion d'Honneur.

In 1835, two Parisienne-born gentlemen, Félix-Joseph Courvoisier and Louis Jules Gallois, Count of Naives, began a joint venture in Jarnac. These two young men had a link to Napoléon through Félix's father, Emmanuel Courvoisier, a wine and spirit merchant who had links with the imperial court. After Napoléon's defeat at the Battle of Waterloo, the ship on which he made his escape lay off the coast of Charentes; Emmanuel ensured that the ship's crew enjoyed plenty of Courvoisier. When Napoléon surrendered to the British, it was the British captain who referred to the stocks of Courvoisier as 'Napoléon's cognac'. This clever strategy on Courvoisier's part (the captain and the crew spread the word about the fine quality of 'Napoléon's cognac') paved the way for an entrance into the English market for the Parisian-based merchant.

In 1852, Félix Courvoisier went into partnership with his two nephews, the Curlier Brothers, expanding the business to become supplier to Napoléon III and laying the foundation for Courvoisier, the cognac house that was to become one of the 'big four' of the future.

MAPPING THE FUTURE

The year 1854 saw the first attempt by officials at mapping the cognac vineyard regions, showing four *crus*: Grande Champagne, Petite Champagne, Première Bois and Deuxième Bois. The second map, in 1870, outlined six *crus*, with the addition of the Fins Bois and Bons Bois regions. Then, as now, there was a discussion about the way in which the areas were to be classified, for it is what is under the surface of the soil that is crucial to *eau-de-vie*, not the name of a town, which is how the regions were originally classified purely for administrative purposes. Yet the earlier map clearly laid out the territory where the best grapes could be grown, and this land became the focus of expansion. More and more houses were established and concentrated on distilling and trading top-quality *eaux-de-vie* – mainly because they reached the best prices.

Throughout the 19th century stocks of *eaux-de-vie* were traded simply. At the market, a seller would present a flask of a sample he wanted to sell, and the buyer would agree a price. The price was set on *eau-de-vie* from the Grande Champagne region; lesser cognacs were, of course, worth less. At one time, the *négociants* met with the middlemen acting as agents for the growers at the restaurant, *Le Coq d'Or*, in the François I square. After meeting and hammering out a deal, the middlemen walked out onto the small balcony and announced the price of the crop to the waiting growers. This was carried out in a gentlemanly manner and relationships were generally amicable.

Yet there was a mood of rebellion among some people. Pierre Salignac, a local grower, cajoled hundreds of growers into forming the United Vineyard Proprietors Company in the late 1830s, as a direct challenge to the Big Three's (Martell, Hennessy and Courvoisier) monopoly of the purchase of the growers' *eaux-de-vie*. The daring move was successful, and soon others copied this concept, launching themselves as merchants. Salignac's move was more than political – he was continually accusing the Martell and Hennessy families of making huge profits at the expense of growers.

The Hennessys (and other houses) were successfully making money, and had moved out of town into the Château de Bagnolet, constructed in 1810 and bought as a family home by Auguste Hennessy (1800 to 1879), senator for the Charente region. The Martell family was already well established in the Château de Chanteloup, located outside Cognac.

THE GLASS REVOLUTION

The 19th century introduced an evolutionary product: machine-made bottles. This new form of trade gave rise to other industries in the region: glassworks, the manufacture of cases and corks, and printing. The man with the see-though touch was one Claude Boucher, whose machine for moulding glass bottles revolutionized the cognac industry. Previously, bottles had been hand-blown, which was arduous work and claimed the lives of many glassblowers, whose lungs were ruined by the effort.

Boucher was a Cognaçais and a local hero (his original machine is displayed just inside the entrance to the museum in Cognac). His glass-making factory opened in 1879 at Saint-Jacques, near Cognac, and his bottle-making machine was invented in 1898. Boucher's work revolutionized the selling and marketing of cognac in export markets, yet not all of the cognac houses bought their bottles from him. Hennessy, for one, sourced its elsewhere.

OPPOSITE: RÉMY MARTIN'S CELLARS REFLECT ON GLASS-LIKE WATER ON A PERFECTLY STILL DAY.

Denis Mounis and Jules Robin were the first to sell cognac in bottles in 1847, exporting them in wooden crates, with their company name emblazoned on hand-printed labels. Following the Free Trade Act of 1860 between France and England, export opportunity rose and so did the merchants' awareness of creating an identity. With the advent of easier and cheaper bottling, it made sense not to send any more anonymous casks for the English merchants and shippers to exploit with their own names.

This decision was not made on a whim, the Cognac and Jarnac merchants banded together and registered their brands under the Trade Marks Act of 1857. Interestingly, Martell claimed to have been branding its cognac with the family

REMY MARTIN

name since the early 1800s – the first-ever label appeared in 1849 on one of its bottles. Hine picked 1817, the year that Thomas Hine changed the name of the company to his own. Hennessy had been using its name only since the middle of the 1850s; the first 'Jas Hennessy & Cie' label appeared on a bottle in 1856.

The Trade Marks Act of 1857 also gave legal protection to cognac companies by setting up a registration system. In a time when cognac from Cognac was considered the best in the world, you could find *conac* in Spain, *conhac* in Portugal and *konyak* in Central Europe. Also, fraudulent shippers from other countries were claiming that their *eau-de-vie* was French – just because it had passed through a French port *en route* to its destination (usually England).

A plethora of stylish and colourful labels were designed, each displaying a company's mark or coat of arms. In 1867, Hine registered its young stag label; in 1864, Hennessy registered its stylized arm-with-axe, while Rémy Martin registered its Centaur seal and patented the Louis XIII carafe. Labels featured bunches of glistening grapes, respectable but scantily clad women, and angels, as well as coats of arms. Usually, the label stated only that the liquid in the bottle was a cognac from a specific merchant.

Branding and labelling were even more important, since companies were broadening their horizons. Cognac was being exported to the United States in 1845, to Australia in 1850, China (the first shipment went from Martell in 1861) and India in 1870. XO – the initials for the blend created by Maurice Hennessy that became world-renowned – was exported to China in 1872, to Russia in 1896 and to Japan in 1900. To establish themselves in these markets, it was essential that cognac houses had one identity the consumer could easily recognize.

Since cognac was a blended spirit, its contents could not be described by one vintage from one vineyard. The answer to the problem of how to describe the age of a bottle's contents allegedly came from an inspiration of Auguste Hennessy. In 1865, he noticed a star embellished on a window latch in his office and created the star system that came to be adopted by the entire industry. At the time of its introduction, a cognac with one star equalled a two-year-old, two stars equalled a four-year-old, and three stars equalled a six-year-old. Simple. For anything older, the word *vieille* ('old') was used. The Hennessy lawyers did not immediately register this star system – De Laage did so in 1868.

Hennessy in particular changed its age-grading system from three stars to VS, VSOP and XO during the next few decades. The initials *VS*, meaning 'Very Special', replaced the three-star appellation after the Second World War, and signify a blend of spirit distilled from the Grande and Petite Champagnes and the Fins and Bons Bois. *VSOP*, by contrast, has royal origins. Back in October 1817, the Prince Regent of England, later George IV, ordered 'a Very Special Old Pale Cognac' from Hennessy; by the end of the 19th century, the initials were on everybody's lips. And cognac further enhanced its well-deserved reputation as the 'spirit of kings'.

The initials XO were first used in 1870, and their origins are still mused upon by those at the Hennessy company. Did the term come from the words 'Extra Old'? Or 'Extraordinary'? Or was it simply called XO because of the markings scrawled in chalk on the casks by the men in the warehouse before they were loaded onto the ship? Typically, XO as a 'logo' was not registered by Hennessy until 1900 in Cognac. By that time, everybody else was using it because it was such an identifiable symbol.

Having established the various standards of cognac on the market with these definitions, consumers were able to understand more about the quality and age of what they were drinking. Export sales campaigns began to reap greater benefits for the producers. Between 1840 and 1872 the Cognac district alone had an average production of 219,000 hectolitres per annum, of which 164,000 were shipped abroad. England took more than 105,000 hectolitres of Cognac's total production.

A glimpse of life in the late 1860s and early 1870s shows a region rich as a result of its international trading and its wealth of natural assets: grapes. New markets were continually being sought – the end of the American Civil War meant that sales to that continent could resume at a higher level – and China beckoned intrepid entrepreneurs such as Hennessy, who delivered their first five casks to Sanghai in 1872.

By the mid-1870s, vineyards covered almost 280,000 hectares of lush Charentais land. But all that would soon disappear with the appearance, in 1872, of phylloxera.

ABOVE: GROWER ANDRE RENAUD WHO BOUGHT REMY MARTIN 200 YEARS AFTER IT WAS FOUNDED. HE DIED IN 1965 AND HIS YOUNGER DAUGHTER INHERITED JUST UNDER 50 PER CENT OF THE SHARES AND MARRIED MAX COINTREAU, WHO LATER BECAME MAYOR OF COGNAC.

PHYLLOXERA & RECOVERY

'Each cognac vintage is similar to a wine vintage. It depends very much on the weather conditions during the year and especially from spring to late summer.'

BERNARD HINE

UP UNTIL THE MIDDLE OF THE 1870S, THE COGNAÇAIS WERE AFFLUENT, TRADE WAS PROSPERING AND THE STOCK LEVELS WERE HIGH. However, with this situation came a complacency which turned out to be a grave mistake. Who could have predicted that such a tiny bug would completely change both the physical and economic landscape of Cognac? And that it would not only affect the landscape, but the taste of cognac in the decades that would follow?

PP126/7: LAST SEASON'S DEAD TENDRILS ARE ENTWINED AROUND SUPPORT WIRES. VINES ARE HARDY CHARACTERS IN ORDER TO SURVIVE ALL KINDS OF WEATHER.

Viticulture, like all aspects of horticulture and agriculture, is prone to a wide range of pests and diseases. Some are nothing more than a nuisance; others can be devastating. Among those that can be classified as devastating are new or unknown pests or diseases, often from a distant part of the world, against which indigenous plant species have no natural resistance. Such a pest suddenly appeared, seemingly from nowhere, in France around 1863. For a decade or more, it threatened the existence of wine production, including that of cognac.

The pest in this traumatic case was *Phylloxera vastatrix*, the vine louse, a small aphid-like insect that had been imported accidentally from the east coast of America into the vineyards of Europe. This little bug fed on the roots of the vines to such an extent that they were killed. The economic future for all vineyards of Europe – not just of France – looked very grim, but fortunately the resourcefulness of man, especially when his business (and hence, his pocket) is hit, is boundless. A solution was eventually found.

In many ways, Cognac was more fortunate that other areas. During the second half of the 19th century, incredible numbers of plants were being introduced into Europe from the New World, in particular from the United States. These plants were of diverse natures: some were used directly in gardens and agriculture, and others were bred with existing species to produce new, more productive crops.

The grapevine, *Vitis vinifera,* existed as a wild plant from Europe and Asia Minor, and had been used for centuries for wine production. However, a large number of other grape species in Northern America were imported into Europe to see whether they could be used to improve native stocks. The trade had progressed in both directions. Settlers and later generations of Americans attempted to grow European vines in America, but failed – mainly, but not exclusively – due to a native aphid that attacked the roots of the vine, cutting off the supply of moisture and nutrients so that the plants died. This yellow aphid was *Phylloxera vitifoliae,* also known as *Phylloxera vastatrix* or as *Dactylasphera vitifolia.* The general condition is still known as phylloxera.

The female aphid burrows into the ground around the roots of a vine. She is tiny (about one millimetre long – only just visible to the naked eye), with flat wings, red eyes and three articulations in the antennae. The aphid lays innumerable eggs near the vine roots, and in just seven to 12 days, the larvae hatch. A few days after this, one and all are positioned on a root, creating

wounds by biting into it, and sucking out the juices. Bacteria and fungi enter the roots through these wounds and infect the plant; rot sets in and the roots swell enormously. Then, three months later, winged nymphs emerge to live on the leaves and buds and to lay more eggs. Some of these climb the vine and are blown by the wind to neighbouring plants or even neighbouring vineyards. Others crawl through the soil, spreading outwards in an ever-increasing circle.

The death of a grapevine attacked by phylloxera is slow and might not be noticed at first. Some die outright, while others may linger on for a few more years. The vines become shrunken, and galls form on the sparse, yellow, withered leaves. As a result, the grapes – if any appear at all – are tiny and sadly entirely useless for winemaking. If unchecked, the original mother vine-louse, who dies after laying her eggs in spring, effectively produces more than 25 million descendants seven months later. Such is the infamy of the phylloxera.

PAGES 130/1: IN LATE WINTER THE VINEYARD MUST BE KEPT NEAT AND TIDY TO PROMOTE MAXIMUM AND SUCCESSFUL BUD-BURST AND FLOWERING BY THE VINES.

These 'yellow perils' not only spread to western America but, with a few exceptions, throughout the rest of the world. According to Denzil Batchelor writing in *The Compleat Imbiber* (Vista Books, 1962), the catastrophic coincidence was that, between 1858 and 1863, the regions of Bordeaux, Roquemaure, and other parts of France had been importing American vines for grafting purposes; it is possible that phylloxera had been brought in on their roots, too.

The first sighting of the aphid in the area was near Roquemaure, and in 1866, infection was reported near Bordeaux. Wine-growers there fought valiantly until giving up in 1880. In 1868, the disease spread to the nearby community of Graveson, where the annual production of wine went from 220,000 gallons

ABOVE: A CARTOON BY FRENCH ILLUSTRATOR GAUTIER, DRAWN DURING THE CRISIS, COMMENTS ON THE PEASANTS' DISMAY AT THE PHYLLOXERA DISASTER.

to 121,000. By 1873, the area produced a mere 1,100 gallons of wine. In 1868, phylloxera was also on the attack in Austria and Hungary; by 1872 it has reached Switzerland, the Rhine and Moselle. In 1876, it began to spread through Madeira, Spain and Portugal. Burgundy came under attack in 1878, and Italy's vineyards followed in 1879. Crete and the Peloponnese were unscathed, as was most of Greece. By 1880, vineyards in South Australia and Victoria were almost destroyed, followed in 1884 by South Africa's Cape region, and Algeria.

Ironically, America remained relatively unscathed, although it was recognized that no imported vine managed to survive more than five years in American soil. Yet the bug still had the urge to travel, and by the 1880s it had arrived in California's vineyards.

The existence of the vine-louse had been reported by Asa Fitch in New York State as early as 1854, and was presumed to have existed for centuries in the Rocky Mountains and the Appalachians. In Britain, the vine-louse was first noticed in 1863, by a scientist named Westwood, in a Hammersmith hothouse, and later the same year in France in two vineyards in the southern Rhône.

By 1867, vineyards in other areas were beginning to report failing vines. As luck would have it, there was no known natural predator in Europe to keep phylloxera under control, nor was there any immunity in the native vines.

By 1884, 67 *départements* in France had been affected in some way. An announcement by M Lalande, President of the Bordeaux Chamber of Commerce, stated that phylloxera had cost France four million – twice the sum exacted by Germany for the Franco-Prussian War. Before the situation was under control, it had wiped out almost 2.5 million hectares of vineyards in France alone.

In Cognac, the phylloxera invasion arrived around 1872 when it was discovered in the roots of vines in the Champagne area. In July of 1874, the area of Jonzac reported no sign of the insect; ten days later it was a different story. The local prefect reported an outbreak in a local vineyard; more villages reported sightings and devastation, and a year later, more than 1,200 hectares had been destroyed. The decade between 1880 and 1890 saw the total devastation of the vineyards of the Grande Champagne *cru*. Those of the three 'Bois' were also affected, but not quite so badly, allowing some production to continue. There were 230,000 hectares in production throughout the Cognac region prior to the plague; today, just 80,000 hectares are planted with vines.

Frantic efforts were made to find a cure for the epidemic. At first, it was not even clear what was causing the problem, and all kinds of reasons were put forward, including over-production and over-pruning, until it was proved conclusively that the yellow louse was the cause. Thousands of suggestions were made as to a cure, some distinctly bizarre while others showed at least some sound reasoning behind them.

What was clear was that the aphids had to be routed our of their second home underneath the leaf and in the root. At first, *vignerons* sprayed the vines with carbon-disulphide and sulpho-carbonate of potassium solutions. These poisonous liquids were injected between the vines, but it was a very expensive process and not very effective. Drowning the pest by flooding the vineyards was the second solution on offer. This was not effective, either.

By the late 1860s, several French scientists were already noting that, on the eastern seaboard of the United States, some vines seemed naturally immune to phylloxera; eventually, the search for a cure moved west to Missouri and later, southwest to Texas. The immune vine species found they were either poisonous to the aphids or their sap was not nutritious enough so that they avoided the disease. The solution for the French wine industry was to rip out all of the European vines and replant with different grapevines grafted on to resistant American rootstock.

The first trials were with *Vitis labrusca*, but this proved unsuitable for the chalky soils on which many of the vineyards are based. The stocks that were eventually brought to Europe were *Vitis riparia*, *Vitis rupestris* and *Vitis monticola*. The *vinifera* scions of the ancient vineyards were dutifully grafted onto these 'colonials' – and still are today. In spite of worries to the contrary, this has had no effect on the resulting grapes, or the wine that is made from them.

OPPOSITE: OH, A VINTNER'S LIFE FOR ME! MODERN TRANSPORT MAKES GETTING ROUND THE HECTARES OF VINEYARDS MUCH EASIER.

THE COGNAC SOLUTION

Cognac was as concerned about the situation as elsewhere in France. Phylloxera first appeared in Crouin in the Charante, and in Chérac in the Charante-Maritime, in 1872, spreading out from there. Fortunately, however, French authorities had already defined the problem before the disease had any great impact on Cognac itself. Government agricultural scientists had already been sent to Missouri to find rootstocks and had imported several million into France.

This was long before it was decided, in 1887, to send viticulturist Pierre Viala to Dennison in Texas where he met the viticulturalist, T V Munson. Eventually, through joint research, the two men succeeded in choosing rootstocks that were suitable for the chalky, dry soils in the Cognac region. Several different types of rootstocks were, and still are, used as they vary according to the type soil of the

crus. In 1988, the 100th anniversary of the 'cure' of phylloxera, Dennison, Texas and Cognac, France became sister cities.

According to Maurice Hennessy, the transformation back to health was a long and arduous process. 'It took five years of experimentation in laboratories to choose a good [rootstock] variety,' he says, 'and afterwards, the evolution was very slow. Remember, there were no mechanical devices – only horses and a man; one man worked the land and production was low. We had no sophisticated chemistry; against mildew, we used only copper and chalk. 'The damage occurred over about 15 to 20 years. In 1870, we had in this area 200,000 hectares of vines; at the end of century, we had only 40,000. It was a disaster.'

Fortunately, prior to the invasion, some merchants had been stockpiling large supplies of cognac, particularly from the good years between 1860 and 1875. One advantage of a long maturation is that stocks from good years help cover those that are lean. However, since there was no known defence against phylloxera, the future for the region still seemed grim, as even the largest stocks would not last for ever. In fact, within a decade, most stocks had gone, and both growers and *négociants* faced ruin.

In 1886, cognac growers and merchants founded the Comité Viticole de l'Arrondissement de Cognac (Viticulture Committee) as a preventitive measure. Four years later, the body approached the French government for support, which led to the creation of the Station Viticole (Viticultural Station), headed by Professor Ravaz. It was the first centre of its kind in France.

By 1898, the new vines were growing well enough to allow the vineyards to replenish the rapidly dwindling stocks. In most of the designated *crus*, the area replanted with vines remained below what it had been before 1875. In other areas, mixed farming, dairy and butter production replaced wine-growing.

The grape varieties used prior to the phylloxera plague had been primarily Colombard and Folle Blanche; afterwards, however, growers used Ugni Blanc (also known as St-Emilion or Trebbiano). This change took place mainly because the Ugni Blanc reacts well to grafting onto rootstock, and is a high-yield grape, very good for distilling, with high acidity. It is also more resistant to other vine diseases, such as powdery mildew and grey rot.

Ugni Blanc originated in Italy, where it was known as Trebbiano, but it was introduced into France as long ago as the 14th century, possibly when the alternative papacy was set up in Avignon. Today, around 95 per cent of grapes grown for cognac are Ugni Blanc with the remainder made up of Folle Blanche and some Colombard.

THE BENEFITS OF PHYLLOXERA

As bad as its effects were, the phylloxera problem had several beneficial results for the region, and for winemaking in general. One was that it caused Cognac to tidy up its old-fashioned methods of planting vines.

'A lot of the soil in some of the vineyards was not very good,' Maurice Hennessy admits, 'and vines had been planted chaotically. Phylloxera changed the way vines had been planted since the 1800s.'

Old photographs of vineyards of this period show many vines planted in a rather haphazard way, often too close to each other (sometimes touching) and certainly not in regular rows. Now, they are almost symmetrical in their layout, planted in rows set five metres (approximately 16 feet) apart. This

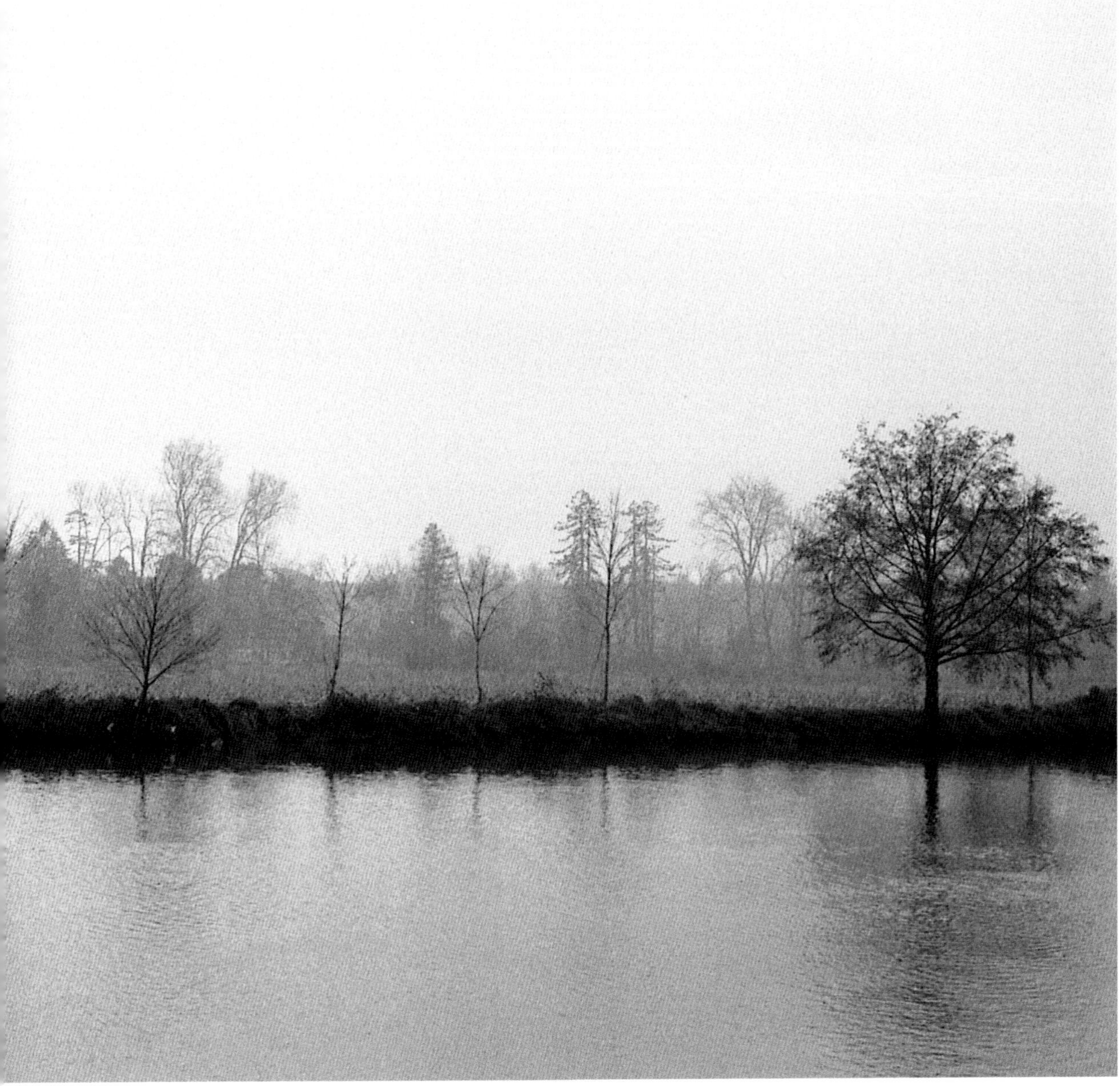

method makes it harder for a bug or other pest to leap from vine to vine, and the roots are not so close together. Ways of harvesting are also very different post-phylloxera. The majority of growers now use machines that straddle and move along the rows, with only a few vineyards still harvesting grapes by hand.

The phylloxera plague had other far-reaching beneficial effects for Cognac. Because of the diminution of supplies of genuine cognac, many vineyards in Europe and far afield, as well as elsewhere in France, promptly filled the yawning gap by producing their own brandy which they unscrupulously labelled 'cognac'. When the genuine cognac stocks began to recover, the real merchants found that they were competing in a market that was saturated with 'fake' products.

'"*It is up to our traders,*" *cried Vivier in 1900, to defend the goodwill of Cognac against the dishonesty and abuse it is subjected to in France and above all, abroad, from the wheeler-dealers and thieves of brand names that pullulate in some countries.*' Taken from *L'Histoire du Cognac*, Robert Delamain (Stock, 1935).

PP140/1: NESTLED AMONG VERDANT LANDSCAPES ALONG THE BANKS OF THE CHARENTE ARE SEVERAL GRAND CHATEAUX.
OPPOSITE: MODERN HORTICULTURAL METHODS ARE APPLIED TO VINES ACROSS THE REGION, WITH SOME PRODUCERS TURNING TO TRADITIONAL ORGANIC METHODS.

The situation was so bad that when the good crops of 1904, 1905, and 1906 arrived, cognac producers did not know if they were going to be able to sell them. Ironically, the most meticulous firms were the first to suffer in the market.

The 1891 Convention of Madrid on copyright of trademarks proposed the general principal that wines named after a 'location' should come only from that region and not to be considered a 'type'. In the case of 'cognac', this should only come from Cognac. But this was merely a declaration of principle, based on honesty. Authority for penalties or sanctions had yet to be defined.

Furthermore, the demarcation of the areas of origin was more than vague. Therefore, one went on drinking *kognak* in Germany, *conac* in Spain, Greek 'cognac' and in France, 'cognac' from all over the country. It took up to 30 years for the principle to work in practice, but in 1909, a decree was issued which defined the area of cognac.

It was essential for the growers in the Cognac region to work together to solve their problems, and they have done so since their recovery from the outbreak of phylloxera. Eventually, they set up a formal organization to control the industry which, in 1946, became known as the Bureau National Interprofessionnel du Cognac, or BNIC. This organization is currently very active, not only in the regulation of the industry but also in its promotion.

There is an yet another interesting side aspect to this tale. If it had not been for the phylloxera plague, British and Americans may not have been introduced to malt and blended whiskies.

OPPOSITE: THE CHARM OF THE LANDSCAPE CREATES A PEACEFUL STATE, YET THOUGHTS OF THE VINE'S PROGRESS ARE NEVER FAR FROM A VINTNER'S MIND.

England had lived on its reserves (even its faint memories) for more than a decade, and had been contemplating a future without cognac. Wholesalers cast about for a substitute, and found it in the form of Scotch. Queen Victoria had drunk it in the Highlands, but records from the time reveal that a mere 38,000 dozen bottles of Scotch were sold in England, as opposed to 83,000 dozen bottles of Irish whisky.

Phylloxera, therefore, was responsible for aiding the development of the Scotch whisky trade in the United Kingdom and the United States.

EXPANDING HORIZONS

'After you make your blend, you put it always in the old barrel to sleep and become aged. And you have just not to shake it. He is an old man. He is living his own life.'

JACQUES RIVIÈRE

THE YEAR 1900 HERALDED THE START OF A NEW CENTURY AND THE START OF A DIFFERENT WAY OF GROWING AND PRODUCING COGNAC. By the turn of the century, vineyards had been completely replanted with new American rootstocks as a result of the phylloxera epidemic. The majority of new vines were Ugni Blanc, which – along with a small amount of Colombard – meant a new style of cognac, one that was less floral and drier. At the beginning of the 20th century, the number of hectares covered by vineyards in the Cognac region was only 40,000 as opposed to the pre-phylloxera figure of 200,000.

PAGES 145/6: IN A CONTEMPLATIVE MOOD, JACQUES RIVIÈRE OF A E DOR CASTS HIS EXPERIENCED EYE OVER THE COLOUR OF ONE OF HIS COGNACS.

The turning of the century occurred in the midst of what we now call *La Belle Epoque* (1898 to 1914). On the picture-postcard surface, Cognac seemed prosperous, yet great challenges lay ahead for both large and small producers. It was the beginning of a tremendous period of change, when technical innovations such as the postal system, electricity, the telephone and the automobile were being introduced to the delight of those who could afford to buy them, facilitating communication with other world markets. Monsieur Henri Frapin purchased his first car, a Panhard-Levassor – a magnificent two-seater affair with leather seats and a mahogany dashboard.

In Cognac itself, a covered market was established in the Place d'Armées, and the Hôtel de Londres sat magnificently in the corner of the town square, with the Café de Londres to the right of the main entrance. Today, alas, the café is gone. One of the first banks, the Credit Lyonnais, was situated on the corner of the square near L'Avenue Victor Hugo. The streets were lined with meccano-like poles carrying electricity (or telegraph wires) around the town. Women bought clothes and fashion accessories at a shop called Aux Dames de France, which hung a sign above its main doors announcing *Entrée libre*. It was an imposing façade, typical of a prosperous town.

Thanks to former mayor Oscar Planat, the *hôtel de ville* (town hall) and its park had become the meeting place on a Sunday afternoon for a recreational walk under the leafy trees by the bandstand. Elegant women wore hats adorned with pretty ribbons. Young girls sported fur-trimmed collars on ankle-length coats. Cheeky boys wore caps pulled forward over their brows.

In 1908, the River Charente was filled with wooden punts and small sailing boats slung low in the water, waiting to be rowed leisurely upstream. The quay by the bridge of Saint-Jacques was a centre of activity, busy with carts unloading barrels, the horses that pulled them waiting patiently for their next task. Bottles in cases stamped with producers' names slid along a plank of timber stretching from quay to merchant ship.

The riverbank sloped right down to the water's edge; the yacht and the rowing club were established in the Parc François I. Regatta days became a social highlight, and women with parasols flirted with both the men and the boys alike. In 1910, the Tour de France cyclists flashed through the town of Cognac, racing around the statue of François I which was protected by black iron railings.

Not everyone was concerned with races or picnics, however, not least the leading cognac houses of the period, for whom business had never been so good. At Hennessy, for instance, formality was the keynote of the workforce. Men wearing stiff collars and ties sat at their individual work stations, dealing with the day's orders. Hennessy had discovered a new way to wrap cognac bottles in wicker baskets that held 30, 40 or 50 bottles. The wicker baskets were then covered in coarse jute cloth, and the whole operation took time and concentration.

Despite its earnest appearance, however, the company was good to its workers. On October 28, 1906, for example, James Hennessy, deputy of Cognac, held a banquet for his employees to celebrate his victory in the elections. The workers turned up for dinner dressed in their best suits to sit at long tables laden with luscious food, bottles of wine, and of course, Hennessy cognac.

By contrast, the cellar at Otard, situated under the Château François I by the riverside, was cavernous and not a little eerie. Huge oak vats neatly lined either side of the room, and the mood was pristine and businesslike as men in bowler hats and formal suits took note of the contents and oversaw the workers.

Another house, the Martell concern, was located on the top of the hill above the quay. Its cognac casks were unloaded outside the company's vast cellar, lifted and rolled from large horse-drawn carts. Once the *eau-de-vie* had been bottled, it was placed in wooden boxes stamped firmly with the Martell name.

The scene at many small-scale producers presented a different picture. At Henri Roy & Co's bottling plant, women sat either on wooden boxes or wooden chairs, labelling their bottles by hand, then wiping them clean, ready to be placed in the export cases. The bottling room at Maison G Bonhomme & Co was also efficient: women were seated at a long table, the bottles lined up for inspection by the foreman. Behind them stood huge vats of *eau-de-vie*. Basic lighting shone down on the workplace. Whether big or small, formal or otherwise, all cognac houses during the 1900s shared the same goal: to produce the best cognac possible and to get the best possible price for it.

A CENTURY OF CHANGE

In addition to competition between whisky and cognac, the early part of the 20th century witnessed open rivalry between the two largest cognac companies, Martell and Hennessy, followed by a period of close cooperation. During the decades that followed, regulations were passed to protect the origin and quality of the product, two world wars began and ended, advertising was developed, the Asian market opened via Singapore, and, in the 1940s, the People's Republic of China's decided to close its doors for 30 years. It was a roller-coaster century of change for any business, and the cognac industry had its own set of peaks and troughs to face.

The cognac trade to Britain had declined as a result of phylloxera. During that period, just as when Napoléon blockaded the shipping lanes, cognac drinkers had turned to whisky. It just so happened that, at the same time, whisky distillers had been working on their single-malt products, blending in a lighter, drier grain whisky to make it more palatable for the general consumer. This new type of Scotch extended whisky's position, not only as an after-dinner tipple, but also as a good mixer: a long drink, a Scotch and water, Scotch and soda, a Chaser, and Scotch on the rocks (an American habit). All of which meant that cognac had to muscle back into the English market aggressively, if it was to muscle back at all. First, however, the merchants had to build up their stocks – which took time.

Cognac merchants were also battling with the outbreak of 'passing off' – the sale of dubious spirits posing as cognac, which took a considerable share of their markets. The main enemy came in the form of brandies from other European countries as well as grain spirits within France itself. In 1903, the Law of March 31 (an update of an 1872 law) stated that all *eaux-de-vie* would continue to be accompanied by documentation relating to their movement from vineyard to destination.

Ironically, many fraudulent imports came from China, a market all cognac merchants were keen to exploit. The major houses, such as Hennessy, expended a lot of energy trying to stop the flood by issuing legal challenges to importers.

In addition to problems with imposter spirits, taxation was still a burden for the cognac companies. In 1909, it was suggested that every bottle of cognac should carry a guarantee, along with the name of the merchant who had made it. On the surface, this looked like a good way to stamp out fraud, but distillers and merchants saw it as a hidden way to extract more tax: it cost an extra 10 *centimes* to stamp each bottle as 'authentic'. Merchants protested vehemently, yet growers were in favour of any move that would deter fraudsters – hence an uneasy conflict of interests developed between the two groups.

PP152/3: A CRITICAL TIME FOR THE DISTILLER – WHEN HE SEPARATES THE HEADS FROM THE TAILS.

In 1929, cognac's special status was formally recognized with the attribution of an *Acquit Jaune d'Or* (Yellow Golden Transport Permit), which set cognac apart from other wines. This permit accompanied the cognac wherever it went as a guarantee of its authenticity. The protection by law only extended to the age of young brandies (up to six years old); there was nothing to guarantee or certify the age of older ones. This situation led to the prohibition of single-vintage brandies, for unscrupulous merchants had been known to pass off brandies from the 1930s as 'Grande Champagne 1811'. A favourite trick was adding younger brandies to a *soupçon* of 1811 that had been languishing in an old cask, then labelling the bottle as 1811. It was not until 1940 that the courts confirmed that age was an integral element in the description of a cognac.

In 1919, however, Courvoisier had invented the advertising slogan 'The Brandy of Napoléon', because of the company's previous association with the emperor. Today the phrase remains firmly entrenched in the corporate vocabulary. To Courvoisier, using Napoléon's name was itself a guarantee of a certain quality – its own answer, perhaps, to the problem of passing off.

THE EFFECTS OF WORLD WAR

The outbreak of the First World War in 1914 took men away from the vineyards, leaving women to do all the farm work, distilling and blending. For this reason, in the trade, the cognac from this year is known as The Year of the Lady, and is renowned for its elegance and bouquet. 'It's not often, in a very macho style of business, that men talk about ladies, so this was an honour,' Bernard Hine told me.

The First World War also meant the closure of the Russian market with the 1917 Revolution, a move that caused financial hardship to one cognac house in particular, Camus. Just prior to the revolution, the company sent a shipment to Russia, which duly arrived; the cheque for payment of two million French *francs* was received, but by the time the cheque made it to the bank for deposit, the Revolution had broken out and it was worthless.

Jean-Paul Camus, current head of the family-owned house, has this cheque framed on his wall. He remembers his father, Michel Camus, talking a lot about the Russian market and the fact that the company had lost a lot of money there. His father was determined, one way or another, to get the money back.

'It was not an easy task at that time with the Russians,' Jean-Paul explained, 'so he made a first visit, a second visit, then a third visit to the Soviet Union and also invited some people to visit us in Cognac.' After four or five years of serious and hard discussions, in 1959 the elder Camus finally signed a contract that gave him the exclusivity for the sale in France of all Russian wines and spirits, and also the exclusivity of exports to Russia of all French wines and spirits.

'That was a very interesting deal that lasted until 1995, until Gorbachev arrived and changed completely the structure of the country,' Jean-Paul observed. 'Through those years, we certainly got our money back, in a different way, but it worked well. And we launched a Russian vodka, Moskovskaya, in France, defining a strict strategy for it and selling it through our distribution networks.' Not all the houses were as inventive in their approaches, however, and many lost fortunes were never recovered.

The end of the First World War brought a short breathing space for the cognac industry at large. However, it also heralded the closure of another market when in 1919 the United States ratified the 18th Amendment and Prohibition began. This presented a unique challenge to the industry. 'Creative paperwork' enabled some stocks to enter the country as medical supplies, complete with import licences. Other stocks went in via Canada, where in 1921, Quebec and British Columbia decided against Prohibition and instead voted in favour of a government licensing system that controlled the sale of alcohol.

To gain more sales, larger houses embarked upon a campaign to seduce drinkers into sipping more cognac. It is generally thought that, by then, the two largest companies, Hennessy and Martell, were used to working with each other; they had certainly been linked by marriage since the 1870. Yet from 1900 to 1920, the Hennessys and the Martells waged what amounted to a ruthless commercial war in all of the territories they were both present in at the time.

Perhaps with the threat of whisky and declining trade in mind, the commercial enmity between Martell and Hennessy came to an end with the signing of an agreement in 1923, whereby the two companies defined their respective territories and consented to share information. The signatures were binding for a period of 29 years, and the agreement aimed not just to protect the product worldwide, but to divide the world into two different but accessible markets. Each company had a shareholding in the other; Martell was to focus on England and Europe, while Hennessy turned its attention to the Far East and the United States.

Hennessy had already spent years concentrating on developing its business in China and South America, appointing local agents to represent the company from 1910. By 1920, China was importing 1,000 bottles a year.

But just as the world was settling down, the stockmarket crashed in Wall Street in 1929, removing the wealth of many a quality cognac drinker. While sales at all houses were affected, the smaller houses specializing in Grande Champagne and Petite Champagne (termed 'Fine Champagne') were hardest hit.

COPING WITH THE GREAT DEPRESSION

The 1930s brought several important events that affected cognac's various international markets. For a start, the British Gold Standard Agreement was broken off by Prime Minister Ramsey MacDonald, the pound was devalued and exports to England rose accordingly. For Courvoisier, a promotional campaign that featured the shadow of Napoléon in its advertisements and publicity material caught the public's imagination just in time for a visit by some 200 spirits merchants to Cognac to see for themselves how much time and care went into the production of one bottle of the regional spirit. If price was a concern, then this, the producers hoped, was one way of explaining the concept of 'time equals money'.

In May 1936, new legislation took the definitions of *terroir* laid down in 1909 and 1919 one significant step further: at last, the word 'cognac' could be used only for spirits produced and distilled in the designated Cognac region. The so-called 'sub-appellations' – Grande Champagne, Petite Champagne, the Borderies, the Fins Bois, Bons Bois and Bois Ordinaires (Bois à Terroir) – were finalized by legislation passed between 1938 and 1978. It seemed that the definition, quality and reputation of cognac were secure at last.

OPPOSITE: A SPIDER'S HEAVEN BUILT AROUND AN OLD GLASS DEMIJOHN IN OTARD'S DARK CELLAR.

THE SECOND WORLD WAR

Despite the new legislation and seeming securing of cognac's future, however, the Thirties also witnessed the occupation of France by German troops. When the Second World War broke out in 1939, the primary objective of those involved in the cognac industry was to save its stock of aged, ageing and young spirits. As the first refugees fled the combat zones, many wound up in Cognac.

At that time, the mayor of Cognac was Paul Firino-Martell. He and his wife, who was president of the Red Cross, took charge of the refugees, arranging housing and temporary hospitals, which were received with gratitude. As a letter from the leader of a convoy of refugees dated 1939 states, 'Cognac is, and will remain the centre of hospitality. It is also the centre of unlimited

charity so characteristic of French people.' In 1940, the German high command requisitioned all cognac stocks. The shippers reluctantly organized a common administrative office to allocate the wines and *eaux-de-vie* of the region to the invading army.

At this time, Martell and Hennessy were still in commercial partnership, and it was agreed that Maurice Hennessy, then president of the Chamber of Commerce, should become the trade's representative to the German troops. The Cognaçais were luckier than many occupied territories; the German in charge of the region was one Gustave Kläebisch, who himself had been born in Cognac and had been Martell's agent in Germany since 1923. His concern was to conserve stocks and maintain the viability of the region's industry.

Back in the mayor's office, Paul Firino-Martell struggled to safeguard Cognac from the civil, administrative and human angles. Everything, of course, was rationed: companies were allowed only so many nails and so much wood apiece – which is why one of Martell's persistent requests was for extra rations for the barrel-makers and loaders.

OPPOSITE: MUCH OF THE CONTINUAL CARE OF COGNAC IS STILL DONE BY HAND AND IN THE TRADITIONAL WAY. HERE A SAMPLE IS TAKEN FROM A VAT.

Meanwhile, Maurice Hennessy was finding his role as go-between increasingly difficult. Given the seemingly endless thirst of the occupying forces, he advised shippers to think themselves lucky if, after the war, they were in a position to start over again. An amazing eight million bottles of cognac were requisitioned by the Germans in 1941, 6.5 million in 1942, nearly eight million in 1943 and four million in the first few months of 1944, before the liberation. Exports, of course, dropped considerably: from around 15 million bottles just before the war to just two million by the end of it.

However, at least Maurice Hennessy's shrewd commercial negotiation skills ensured that the Germans paid well for their acquired taste; a solid financial structure remained in the background, which proved to be a source for renewal when the war was over.

Ask *négociants* about these war years and there is a slight pause while they reflect upon how they ought to reply. One thing is clear: they were not going to give up their precious commodity easily. There are tales of false walls being built to hide stocks in the cellars, made to look as if they had been there for years. In addition, the nearby region of Segonzac harboured miles of underground caves, especially behind the house of Croizet, where cognac producers hid their stocks. The only problem was that the caves provided a wet environment and therefore too much water developed in the ageing cognac.

According to Philippe Eymard of Croizet, there were also plans for a top secret aircraft to be constructed in these caves under the very noses of the Germans. Eymard told me an amusing story of an incident during the war in which his father had shown a remarkable sense of spirit. A German limousine drove in through the old iron gates that mark the entrance to Croizet's property. Two German soldiers got out and approached his father.

'We are from Göring's staff in the Netherlands,' they barked, 'and we would like to have your best cognacs'.

'But that's impossible!' the elder Eymard replied. 'My best stocks were on the docks at Bordeaux, and Göring bombed the docks yesterday, so I am not able to give them to you.' And that was the end of the matter.

WAR'S END – AND BEYOND

In 1944, the airbase in Cognac was evacuated by the German troops, who partly destroyed it despite attempts by local officials to limit the damage. The reconstruction of the airbase, achieved by a contribution of five million *francs* on behalf of the cognac shippers, was carried out quickly for the imminent arrival of General de Gaulle, who was due to visit his troops in September 1944. The base became the headquarters of the general staff of the Atlantic Air Forces.

The war finally ended for the Cognaçais on May 8, 1944, but while the German menace had ended, things did not exactly run smooth for the producers. For one thing, a disastrous frost reduced the year's harvests to just 24,000 hectares. In addition, the spread of whisky through the United States meant that cognac merchants had to quickly adopt a more aggressive stance in the world spirits market if they were to regain their lost ground.

In September 1949, yet another blow fell on cognac's future, with a decision by the People's Republic of China to end all imports for the next 30 years. A huge market had dried up without warning, and producers were hard-pressed to find new ones that would take its place.

Fortunately (if that is indeed the right word), the deprivations of the war years had created a society keen to indulge in luxury goods – and due to its associations with emperors, kings and invading armies, cognac symbolized the epitome of luxury. From the 1950s onward, the French spirit became synonymous with status, setting a style its makers hoped would last for decades to come.

AN EMERGING GIANT

'What is rare justifies the price. You have to put it in the right environment. You don't serve caviar on a plastic plate.'

MAURICE HENNESSY

THE GOLDEN PERIOD JUST AFTER THE WAR YEARS WAS FUELLED BY THE GROWTH OF MARKETS PREVIOUSLY ON HOLD, SUCH AS THE UNITED STATES AND ENGLAND.

Just how cognac became to be associated with wealth, glamour and the traditional cigar-smoking male environment is related in part to the upper-class British market that developed during the 1800s. It was developed further in the United States by Hennessy's appointment of a public-relations company headed by Edward Gottlieb, who, by working with high-end magazines, established a top-quality image.

PP164/5: THE GRAND HENNESSEY BUILDING, WITH NEW VISITOR CENTRE DESIGNED BY J M WILMOTTE.

During the 1950s, cognac was also viewed as an ideal cocktail beverage, advertised by houses large and small as a spirit perfect for mixing with tonic or soda. In the United States, cognac and ginger ale was a popular drink; many cognac-based cocktails were also still in demand, including the Brandy Alexander, the Sidecar, the Champagne Cocktail and an interesting little innovation known as Between the Sheets. Cognac was also drunk with water, and it was the Americans who introduced the concept of cognac 'on the rocks'.

Even so, Scotch whisky was still cognac's main competitor – and it was cheaper. Price had always been a determining factor in the positioning of cognac. The cost of producing one bottle of cognac is much higher than that required to produce a bottle of whisky. Cognac cannot and probably never will be as cheap as whisky: hence its love affair with a quality image.

In an attempt to reinforce its appeal as a luxury product, cognac packaging became more luxurious, and the advertising campaigns more unique. Decanters, filled with cognac of XO quality and upward, were already a feature of the oriental market. Even now, such decanters are glamorous, and each house vies with the other to be more seductive at this level. Rémy Martin has its Louis XIII, Hennessy has Richard Hennessy, Camus has Jubilee, Frapin has Extra, and Courvoisier has long boasted its hand-painted Erté Collection. The latter are now out of production and are considered collector's items. Other houses tried to outshine each other, literally, by commissioning glass decanters glinting with gold.

During this same period, each of the cognac companies, whether large or small, decided upon which niche of the market they were aiming for, and worked towards retaining it.

THE LURE OF THE EAST

In the early 1960s, Michel Camus commissioned a market study which revealed that the three-star market was in the hands of Hennessy, Martell and Courvoisier – against which most smaller houses could not fight. Yet this left other qualities of cognac, such as premium labels, to be exploited by smaller houses in the various markets. It was this niche market that Camus took as its goal.

According to the son of Michel Camus, Jean-Paul, 'Asia was then an emerging market, a place where VSOP cognac was drunk. My father decided we were going to go beyond VSOP and get into this market with Napoléon. Asians had more and more money, and they were looking to buy such products.'

Camus also realized the huge potential of the Far East duty-free business – a shrewd move at a time when few other cognac companies even recognized duty-free as a market. Camus cultivated a close relationship with its duty-free customer, a Pacific-based company called DFS, then built upon that base to reach the Asian domestic markets, which are still huge consumers today. Japan is a case in point – in 1988 the country imported 10 times more cognac, in volume terms, than Italy.

Courvoisier's marketing strategy was also inspired. Its president at the time was Christian Braastad, from a Norwegian family who had settled in Cognac. Braastad's strategy was, first, to promote the association with Napoléon in a new frosted bottle on the French market and, secondly, to double the company's export efforts. He also began to buy stocks only when they were required, which meant that both stock levels and the cash supplies were reduced. By the 1960s, Courvoisier was looking for a buyer – which is how Canadian company Hiram Walker bought into the luxury spirit market.

OPPOSITE: HENNESSY'S OLD COGNACS KEPT UNDER LOCK AND KEY IN THEIR BEAUTIFUL PARADIS.

Other takeovers and mergers had either taken place or were in the air during the 1960s and early 1970s. Cognac became a desirable luxury addition to a spirit company's brand portfolio. Hine, for example, was purchased by the whisky company Distillers Company Limited in 1971. This era of mergers signalled the beginning of the trend for major decisions about cognac to be made outside the region that bore its name.

The 1973 oil crisis forced producers to focus their attentions on the United States. Then (as now) consumption of cognac in the United States was confined mainly to the male ethnic market, who had a preference for VS and three-star cognac. The United States also proved to be an important market for high-end houses such as Hine, which produces only cognacs of VSOP quality and above. Hine first exported to the United States during the first half of the 19th century.

As a producer of quality aged cognacs (Triomphe is a 45-year-old-blend), Hine is also one of the few companies also allowed to produce 'vintage' cognac. In 1963, due to growing fraud, growers and the Bureau National Interprofessionnel du Cognac (BNIC) agreed that no cognac house could reserve stocks from each vintage. This agreement lasted until 1989, when it was decided that, if documentation were correct, a cask could be placed in a company's special bonded *chai* for long ageing. In the case of Hine, they hold one set of keys to the cellar, the BNIC the other set, so there can be no doubt about the authenticity of what is in the cask. Today, part of Hine's success is due to its practice of educating wholesalers and those who work in the bar business about its products, including how they are made and aged.

Delamain is another company that specializes in ageing and bottling vintage cognacs. It agrees with the Hine philosophy that putting casks away for future generations is an essential part of the cognac business. Delamain also jealously guards its independence. For over 300 years, it has built a worldwide reputation as the Rolls Royce of the cognac industry. It was one of the few houses to ship early-landed cognacs into Bristol for ageing because English dampness is an important aspect of its pale, dry style of cognac. Considering that giants such as Bacardi, Seagram, Pernod-Ricard and Suntory have all purchased a cognac house, independents such as Delamain must feel as if they are besieged. Charles Braastad-Delamain, in his early 30s, is the latest family member to join Delamain. He is determined to carry on the family's strong tradition of high-quality cognacs – despite competition from the big multinationals. 'We are cognac people, not marketing people,' he says. 'Give us a glass of distilled cognac and we can tell you if the making of the wine and its distillation was well done: we have the Delamain nose.'

Braastad-Delamain's grandfather was chairman of Courvoisier, which is why as a child, the young Charles used to meet all the Courvoisier agents when they came to the house for lunch or dinner. This friendly way of doing business has changed, and Courvoisier, along with the other large houses, doesn't operate like that anymore. The people who run the companies may not stay in Cognac for longer than it takes for them to move one more rung up the corporate ladder – an attitude that had its beginnings in the 1970s.

THE TROUBLED ERA

During the 1970s, the planting of vineyards in the Cognac region was rigorously controlled. There was a demand from shippers to 'double the vineyards and double the sales', but the small growers and grower-distillers felt this was a move designed to bring down the price of *eau-de-vie*.

In late summer of 1971, representatives of wine-growers and representatives of the *négociants* met before the harvest, to agree the price at which the *négociants* would buy the new crop. Where before, the meeting had been an amiable affair, this time it was different. Since the Asian market was proving so successful, the wine-growers wanted a share of the boom-time profit; that summer, they held out for a better price. To support their representatives during the negotiations, about 500 growers demonstrated outside the BNIC, where the discussions were being held. They didn't get exactly the price they wanted, but the outcome was reasonable. At the end of the meeting, however, a small fracas occurred when Michel Camus, a representative of the *négociants*, left the meeting and got into his car. He was surrounded by protestors and the car was shaken by the crowd. A wine-grower whom he did not know recognized him and stepped forward to ask his fellow protestors to let him go, which they did.

'One week later, Michel Camus' saviour paid a visit to the office, reminding him of the incident,' recalled Jean-Paul, Michel Camus' son. 'From his pocket, he took a sample of cognac from his estate, and of course, my father bought his batch. The wine-grower has since become a regular supplier to Camus.'

This story emphasizes the strength of relationships in this business, both at home and in overseas territories. The Cognaçais have always been great travellers. During the 1970s (just as today), a typical Monday morning at the local railway station would find the major players gathered, waiting for a train to take them to Paris and beyond to nurture important commercial friendships.

In 1974, however, it was a local event that dominated the merchants' interests, when a spectacular fire at one of the Martell warehouses astonished the town. Casks flew through the roof, and rivers of blazing brandy flooded the warehouse, eventually flowing into the river.

The smell of *eau-de-vie* reached far into the surrounding countryside, drifting up from the river where the alcohol settled; owing to the lack of rain in the region, it moved no more than a few hundred yards per hour, and dead fish littered its surface. Enough cognac to fill half a million cases was destroyed that

ABOVE: COGNAC AWOKE TO THE SOUND OF BARRELS FLYING THROUGH THE ROOF AS FLAMES ENGULFED THE MARTELL AGEING CELLARS IN 1974 – SOME SIX MILLION WORTH OF STOCK WAS DESTROYED.

fearful day, at the equivalent cost of six million pounds. While the Martell employees were understandably horrified, a comment from the company's agents in the United Kingdom at the time put the loss into a strange type of perspective. 'Though it has to be replaced, demand has slackened off recently,' he said. This, sadly, was the situation for all other cognac producers, as by the close of the decade, cognac had gone into a slump.

DECADES OF DESPAIR

During the 1980s, another threat to cognac sales emerged in the form of vodka. The clear spirit was rediscovered by young and old alike in bars and clubs, part of the culture that developed during the 'era of conspicuous consumption'. Champagne still held the high ground on the wine scene, but the snobbish, traditional macho image attached to cognac the 'after-dinner-drink' effectively removed it from view.

The start of the next decade offered little hope. Cognac producers would probably prefer to forget 1990, when the BNIC announced what must have been the smallest harvest of the century. The situation did not improve greatly over the next few years. In 1991, the American market – at the time, the world's second-largest importer of cognac, after Japan – dropped 37.9 per cent in volume and 24.9 per cent in value.

This situation, caused by market stagnation, was made worse by the precautionary action taken by shippers in late 1990. Fearing that cognac was a prime target for tit-for-tat reprisals by the United States as a result of open conflict between the European Union and the United States over maize subsidies, extra stocks of cognac had been shipped across the Atlantic.

When the reprisals never materialized, America was overstocked with cognac. Meanwhile, demand in Europe also declined, but in Asia, sales rose, with Japan dominating the market. Then, however, in 1991, disaster struck when the Asian market collapsed.

The last five years of the 1990s were also slow for cognac sales, due to worldwide economic recession. Global sales plummeted, and the domestic market fell to an all-time low. When China regained possession of Hong Kong in 1997, a new set of political positionings had to be dealt with. The 1997 Asian crisis did nothing to ease the situation, nor did the abolition of duty-free sales in Europe in 1999.

Not surprisingly, growing discontent between growers and *négociants* came to a head in the late 1990s, when the town of Cognac was blockaded with tractors, trailers, burning tyres and flaming casks of brandy. Growers claimed they did it to protest their concern that the big companies were not buying enough of their produce, and vent their anger over the fact that the global taste for cognac seemed to have all but disappeared. The French government's reaction was to provide grants for the growers to pull up their vineyards.

Aside from the blockading of Cognac, however, the collapse of the spirits markets was not confined solely to cognac. Other spirits were affected, too, particularly malt whisky. This downturn in spirits consumption as a whole coincided with a resurgence of interest in drinking and mixing exotic, sometimes classic, cocktails. Yet as an industry, cognac producers lost the opportunity to access the growing 'cocktail culture' and in effect, let whisky producers walk all over them. What the marketing people didn't see coming was that there would be also be a move back to lighter products, related to a new desire on the part of consumers to adopt a more health-conscious lifestyle.

A RETURN TO STYLE

Whatever the reasons for the decline in cognac sales, however, radical action was and still is necessary. Hennessy, Courvoisier and Martell are each determined to make cognac desirable again, by associating it with fashion and competing with vodka in the bar and clubbing markets. Each of these companies is targeting what (in marketing-speak) are known as the modern independents: young adults aged between 28 to 35 with plenty of disposable income. Recent research indicates that these consumers order by brand. They don't ask for a simple Vodka Martini; they ask for a Martini made with Absolut or Stolichnaya.

In September 2000, for example, Courvoisier launched itself in the United States with a chic campaign in United States *Vogue* magazine, as the 'House of Courvoisier'. The four-page advertisement shows a bottle of cognac on the front page only; other pages depict a diamante brooch against red sequins, a pair of pale leather boots stamped with the shadow of Napoléon, and on the last page, a skimpy evening top gleaming with gold chains. Courvoisier created the campaign to present a premium image. Like other multinationals, it wanted to regain cachet, target the urban consumer and reintroduce the concept of mixed drinks.

OPPOSITE: CHARLES BRAASTAD-DELAMAIN STUDIES WITH HIS 'NOSE' EACH DAY ALONGSIDE HIS FATHER TO LEARN THE NUANCES OF THE DELAMAIN COGNAC STYLE. .

Similarly, in the March 2001 *Harper's Bazaar* (United States edition), a full-page advertisement for Hennessy was the only spirit ad in the entire magazine, rubbing shoulders with the likes of fashion houses such as Prada, Gucci, Ralph Lauren and Hermès.

Despite the downturn in cognac consumption during the 1980s and 1990s, in 1998, Seagram, the United-States-based spirit giant, bought Martell for two

reasons. First of all, Seagram didn't have a cognac house as part of its portfolio. Secondly, and probably equally important, the company wanted to take advantage of the Asian distribution channels that the Martell family had so shrewdly developed.

In Seagram's corporate opinion, shrinking demand simply meant a chance to grab market share; in addition, the company recognized that cognac's core consumer base was ageing. The traditional image of cognac consumption was of gentlemen holding balloon glasses and cigars, seated in high-backed leather chairs in the depths of some dark, oak-panelled bar – certainly not the type of spirit to interest a younger generation. Yet it is precisely the younger generation that Seagram wanted to target. Added to that, however, is an older female consumer who drinks VS and VSOP cognacs; she must not be alienated to the product via any image change.

OPPOSITE: THE BEAUTIFUL CHATEAU PLEISSES, NEAR COGNAC, IS HOME TO THE CAMUS FAMILY.

With the recent merger of Seagram and Pernod-Ricard, there is an air of uncertainty in both London and Cognac. Many in Cognac viewed the acquisition by Seagram as a disaster for Martell. In 1988, there were 800 staff; now there are only 400. Output, too, has declined less. One master-blender stated bluntly, 'Seagram has ruined Martell.' Yet it is all a matter of opinion.

Martell, meanwhile, has tried to cope with the image problem of cognac by developing its 'Meet Martell' campaign, part of which involves an Italian model who represents the company. At 26 and with the ability to speaks five languages, the model portrays a truly international image. Her role is more than looking sexy and elegantly mischievous – she is the public face of Martell, travelling the world, meeting agents and talking to the media.

Tastes have changed and cognac has to change with them, if it is to survive. Hennessy created Pure White as a new blend to satisfy the demand for a fresher flavour. Most VS and VSOP cognacs are lighter in colour, and feature a hint of dryness that is good for mixing cocktails or long drinks. With this in mind, Rémy Martin has launched Rémy Red and Rémy Silver (cognac mixed with vodka), which have been blended for the younger palate, while Camus has launched its Néon cognac in a trendy tall, thin bottle.

There is also no doubt that cognac has been 'feminized', now that femininity and fashionable sensuality sell cognac via the global conglomerates. There is also a new female market: at least a third of patrons of quality bars are female, more than ever before. Women are making their mark in business and becoming connoisseurs in their own way. This is definitely a growing niche that needs to be explored. Another niche market exists in the United States. There, cognac is largely drunk by black male consumers aged over 40, with high incomes and established careers, who want to show they can afford the good things in life.

WHAT THE FUTURE HOLDS

Lined up alongside the multinationals, the Bureau National Interprofessionnel du Cognac (BNIC) sits on an uneasy fence representing both the global companies and the traditional producers to the French government. The BNIC puts forward a common strategy for the promotion of cognac throughout the world, yet increasingly, the global companies follow their own marketing strategies. Often a marketing decision, taken in New York, is not even relayed to the sales and marketing department in the cognac house concerned. This makes it hard for the houses, and harder for the BNIC to keep track of the images being presented.

Yet even within the BNIC itself, images are changing. Claire Coates is the organization's director of communications (a female director in what was, until recently, an industry dominated by men) and she is continually looking to launch new products. Courvoisier's *Vogue* spread doesn't amaze her in the slightest.

'It's a natural evolution,' she says. 'Cognac has always been considered a serious product. But it is also important to be accessible, so we must offer accessibility without losing our soul, or identity; producers are looking to fit their products into this trend. Society is changing; people want more fun in their lives. Showing cognac as seductive, as fashionable and sensual, means it is seen as a pleasure.'

The BNIC has a simple and yet difficult aim: to promote cognac's image worldwide. Its role is to protect and promote, because cognac is a unique product made in a specific way. The organization is well aware that most people think of it as synonymous with brandy, it is necessary to explain why cognac is different.

Cognac now has a split personality: the purist producers of exquisite XO, Grande Champagne and Fine Champagne cognacs pale at the thought of adding a mixer to their products, especially if that product is aged 15 years or over. Other producers are buying into the new marketing strategies as a way of selling surplus spirit. After all, if the majority of the market is VS and VSOP, then adding it to ice, a dash of soda or tonic, or creating cocktails using other spirits and fruit juices cannot be that sacrilegious. I, for one, do this every day in the bar. But adding a dash to cognac the quality of Napoléon, XO or Extra is considered a crime in some quarters.

There are many different qualities of cognac to suit individual tastes, and with the blending knowledge now available, it should be possible for a company to easily straddle both worlds. As one of the master-blenders I met on my last trip stated, 'I produce the product. Who am I to tell consumers how to drink it?'

2

THE END OF THE JOURNEY

I WANT TO SHARE WITH YOU MY PASSION FOR VINTAGE COGNACS. AS YOU WILL HAVE LEARNED FROM READING THE EARLIER CHAPTERS, THE CREATION OF COGNAC TAKES PLACE OVER A NUMBER OF YEARS. This incredible process is carried out by honourable people with a timeless agenda, since time is the key element to a great cognac.

P182/3: A LINE OF SAMPLES THAT MIGHT GO INTO A PARTICULAR BLEND ARE LABELLED AND STORED IN THE TASTING ROOM.

During my journeys to Cognac, I have met some of the industry's greatest characters, all of whom are cognac experts. From them I have learned the subtle nuances that may be found in a grand old cognac. My friend Bernard Hine put it succinctly when he said, 'Not all women can afford to go to Dior, yet everybody is going to talk about what Christian Dior has been doing in its last fashion show – which is the same for vintages. You have to understand that vintages are our milestones, our memories of the past.'

My own personal memories are of ancient golden cognacs, as lively as the day they were bottled. Uncorking them is always an emotional experience, especially if they are from an historic year. This brings to mind the story of Winston Churchill, England's wartime hero, who, when given a glass of vintage Bual 1792 during a visit to Madeira, cried out, 'Do you realize, gentlemen, that when this wine was made, Marie-Antoinette was still alive?' It is this tremendous, tingling excitement and anticipation that I try to pass on to a guest when I open a bottle of vintage cognac in the bar. For me, the magic never fails to work. It is as if it is part of the spirit itself. Here, you can read about the vintages I have tasted during the last 20 years, along with some of the amusing incidents that have happened to me during this period.

I also include notes on my favourite cognacs currently on the market. To help guide you through these notes – particularly when words such as *rancio* make you shake your head in wonder – I offer advice on how to approach tasting a Grande Champagne cognac. You can use this system to taste any other cognac, such as a Fine Champagne or an XO, as similar flavours will be found in them (but not in quite such an intense way).

Cognac is not about alcohol; it is about perfume. You must close your eyes and concentrate on the aromas you are accustomed to every day of your life and can easily recognize in your aroma memory-bank.

Advice on how to store and serve cognac is also given, and if there are terms I have used that are unfamiliar to you, turn to the glossary on page 264. I have included the latest statistics from the Bureau National Interprofessionnel du Cognac on sales and territories. These figures reveal that 60 per cent of cognac consumption is drunk as a mixer such as soda water, fruit juice, or tonic, or on ice. To me, this reinforces how unique the other 40 per cent (the highest-quality cognacs) are, those that are drunk purely as *digestifs*.

In this world of quick returns, we must not lose sight of the fact that the finest cognac, this noble spirit, is liquid gold. To me, it is worth every *franc*, dollar or pound it costs to enjoy.

GRANDE CHAMPAGNE
1805
A EDOR
SOLEIL
D'AUSTERLITZ

MEMORABLE MOMENTS

'The difference between cognac and armagnac? Imagine a length of velvet and another of silk fabric. Stroke them. The velvet has a deep and rich texture, and that is an armagnac. The silk is pure finesse, and that, to me, is a cognac.'

SALVATORE CALABRESE

WHEN YOU LOOK AT A PAINTING BY PICASSO, YOU CAN SEE THE ART OF CREATION. WITHIN A VINTAGE COGNAC LIES THE UNSEEN ART OF DISTILLATION.

To many people in the world of cognac, the word 'vintage' is merely a distraction from the main business. It represents, after all, just one per cent of all production in a marketplace that is dominated by blends.

P186/7: A PRECIOUS DEMIJOHN IN A E DOR'S PARADIS RESTS AMONG THE COBWEBS, HOME OF THE WOOD-WEEVIL MUNCHING SPIDER THAT FEASTS ON THE CASKS.

Yet to me, the vintage aspect is at the very heart of the passion that started me on my journey into the world of cognac. It was through the discovery of rare vintage cognacs that I developed the concept of liquid history. It began when I was seeking an idea that would make the small bar at Duke's Hotel, a well-kept secret off St James's in the centre of London, the centre of attention.

One day, while staring out of the window, I realized the answer was literally right in front of me: the stone courtyard outside the hotel was centuries old and steeped in history. Turning away from the window, a painting of the Duke of Wellington, dated 1815, caught my eye. People have always said the bar at Duke's was haunted; the last concierge swore he used to see an old gentleman sitting in a chair in the far corner of the bar by the window. I cannot claim to have seen this ghostly spectre, but I always felt his presence and felt he must have been looking after me. The more I looked at the duke, the more I thought that perhaps he was trying to tell me something – London, full of history; imagine the year 1815, the brilliant Battle of Waterloo; despatches rushed to Westminster and to the Court of St James....

It doesn't really matter how far we go into the future, we are still somehow enamoured of the past. There I was, surrounded by fantastic antiquities rare in a society obsessed with trendiness and modernity. I could touch them, see them – but one thing was missing in the world of spirits around me. I didn't have one bottle on the shelf behind the bar that I could give to people in order for them to 'taste history'. From that moment on, I began my research into great moments in political and military history, starting with the Duke of Wellington and the Battle of Waterloo. I also began searching for a liquid I could sell as a sip of history.

It couldn't be an old bottle of vintage wine because that has a limited life. Once you open it, the taste alters as it comes into contact with the air. So it had to be an *eau-de-vie*, such as cognac. I had always been fascinated by the complexity of this spirit, and hoped that a traditional wholesaler would be able to guide me in the right direction.

The key challenge was to match an historic event with a bottle of vintage. The next step was to find a rare bottle of vintage cognac. Where to start? I searched auction-house catalogues, old liquor stores, spoke to owners of private cellars. There is an old Italian saying: 'By asking the way, you will reach Rome.'

Ask one person, and that conversation leads to another, and another, and gradually a synergy happens. For me, a bottle of 1812 vintage cognac immediately conjures up Napoléon's retreat from Russia. Some 550,000 troops went into Moscow, and only 20,000 returned. Think of that. At the same time, the British were at war with the United States over naval policy. The cognac in that particular bottle has survived over 200 years.

Yet the biggest challenge is not relating such a vintage to history so much as deciding whether or not to open it and admire it for its complexities. Most vintage collectors perceive the value of their purchases in their entirety – not in an empty bottle. To me, however, the most important aspect of that 1812 bottle is the liquid inside it – not the complete package. The cognac, distilled in that period, is asleep, and needs to be awakened, like Sleeping Beauty in the classic fairy tale.

Peter Gray, then at Whitwham's in Chester, was responsible for my first close encounter with a vintage cognac. It was in 1984. I bought a bottle of 1914 Hine for the bar at Duke's. It was an emotional moment. In my hands was a rare bottle, and it represented the beginning of my journey. As stated in Chapter 7, the year 1914 is known in the cognac trade as 'The Year of the Lady', since the men were fighting in the First World War and women worked the fields, planting and harvesting the grapes, as well as distilling the *eaux-de-vie*. Once the regular cognac-lovers were told the story of its liquid history, this cognac 'sold out' within a week. The empty bottle reassured me that my concept of selling liquid history was right on the mark.

Not long afterwards, via Bernard France, a private collector, I found a bottle of 1789. Since then, I have had the pleasure of tasting an 1805, 1815, 1820, 1834, 1844, 1853... something, in fact, from every decade of the 19th century right through to the early 1970s. Hence I began to gain a reputation for having the most expensive palate in the world.

ABOVE: THE SEA PORT OF LA ROCHELLE WAS A BUSY TRADING POST DURING THE 18TH CENTURY, WITH BOTH WINES AND COGNAC LOADED FOR HOLLAND, ENGLAND AND SCANDINAVIA.

Yet besides a love of history, there is another aspect to this passion of mine. Any cognac produced before 1872/73 has been made with pre-phylloxera grape varieties, such as Colombard and Folle Blanche. For me, this represents a taste of grapes that are descended from the same rootstock originally planted by the Romans. A pre-phylloxera cognac tastes much more intense, more floral, with a hint of chocolate and a sweetness on the finish. To taste a cognac from these years – well, all I can say is that it is a moment to savour.

I prefer to share rare bottles with as many people as I can, which is why I make it a house policy not to sell a second glass from the same bottle to the same guest. I explain that they can experience another moment in time through sipping another year, and most are usually happy to do so. The current collection of 75 bottles in the bar at The Lanesborough Hotel in London, where I work, includes a Courvoisier 1824, a Bignon 1800 (from the cellar at Maxim's in Paris) and a Massouges 1810.

These days, my personal collection numbers over 300 empty bottles, most of them dating from the 1700s onward. Whenever I come near to the end of a bottle, I never sell it all, preferring to leave a small *soupçon* in the bottom.

VINTAGE MOMENTS

OVER THE 18 YEARS OR MORE THAT I HAVE BEEN OFFERING VINTAGE COGNAC, A WIDE RANGE OF PEOPLE HAVE BEEN INTRODUCED TO ITS FINESSE. Sometimes, they want to commemorate an occasion – an anniversary, for instance, or just a special meeting. In this section, I would like to share a few of these 'moments' with you.

The first time I met Jacques and Bernard Hine, they were brought to the bar at Duke's for an aperitif by a Mr Crosby, at the time a director of Johnnie Walker who were interested in representing Hine in London. After lunch,Crosby asked me to come through to the restaurant and requested three glasses of fine Hine Antique. 'I have something a little better to offer you,' I replied, and walked away.

Now, Crosby is a large and powerful man. He looked startled and began to go red in the face with a mixture of rage and embarrassment. There I was, seemingly endangering his big pitch to the Hines. Those few minutes that I was away from the table must have seemed like an eternity to him.When I returned, I did have a bottle of Hine Antique, but I also carried a bottle of Hine 1928 vintage cognac. 'I thought it would be appropriate to show you this,' I said, and presented, with a flourish, the 1928 vintage, which impressed them a little.

Then I showed them my *coup de grace*: a rare bottle of Hine 1844. At this point, both Bernard and Jacques rose from their dining chairs, amazed. Even they had not seen a bottle of this cognac during their time at Hine. Meanwhile, Crosby's demeanour changed instantly. How could I not give them a sip of the 1844?

The late Maurizio Gucci was also a guest at the hotel. Once, he asked me to find a bottle of 1927 to celebrate the acquisition of a beautiful yacht that had been built in that year. It took me some time, but I did find one and kept it until he came back to London.

Another guest came to the Lanesborough bar specifically for a taste of liquid history, having heard about the collection from a business colleague. I finished my presentation with a bottle of Maison de l'Empereur 1802, which had two to three glasses left in the bottle. I asked him to think about some of the events that occurred in that year: Napoléon was embarking upon his Italian strategy; Thomas Jefferson was the newly elected president of the United States. At the mention of Jefferson's name, the man's face lit up; Jefferson was his political hero. 'That,' he said, 'is the cognac I want to taste.'

P194/5: THIS USEFUL SMALL HAMMER IS USED BY THE MAITRE DE CHAIS TO GENTLY KNOCK OUT THE BUNG OF THE BARREL, CAUSING MINIMUM DISTURBANCE, WHEN SAMPLING.

The American singer Michael Bolton had been staying in the hotel but had not visited the bar. In the foyer, I asked him why. He replied, 'You probably don't have Hennessy Paradis, my favourite cognac' – or words to that effect. This, of course, was like a red rag to a bull. I asked him to step inside the bar. Not only did he see his favourite cognac, he was also introduced to the vintage collection. Within half an hour, Bolton was sniffing, tasting and sipping some of the rarest cognacs in the world. He's developing into quite a good connoisseur I believe.

In December 1990, I had the privilege of serving Her Majesty Queen Elizabeth II with a bottle of Pascal Combeau & Co 1926, the year she was born, during a private dinner at Duke's Hotel. Lord Westbury, who organized the affair, asked me to find this special year, suggesting that it could be drunk after dinner as the perfect end to the evening. As customary, one always offers it to Her Majesty first. I approached her with the bottle of 1926 in my hands and asked if she wanted a glass of cognac. Initially, she declined graciously, without looking at the label. Determined not to let this moment pass, I asked tentatively, 'Ma'am, may I introduce you to a great year for a great lady?' and presented the bottle to her so that she could read the date. She recognized it, smiled, and consented to a glass.

Clint Black, an American country and western singer, shares my enthusiasm for vintage cognacs, and his own collection contains some rare bottles. It began when he tasted a glass of 1805, and since then, we have enjoyed many collectors' moments together. However, one of the most tragic involved an imperial-size bottle (it stands almost two feet, six inches high and holds the equivalent of eight bottles) of Hennessy Grande Fine Champagne 1857. This was one of the largest bottles I had ever come across. I bought it from a Swiss collector and had it shipped to Black in California. It arrived in one piece, and he created a special display case for it as the focal point of his collection.

Unfortunately, unfortunate things do happen with vintage cognac. After a year or so, Black noticed that the cork had shrunk and fallen into the bottle. The lead seal, however, was still intact. He called me for advice and I asked him if he knew of a wine merchant who could solve the problem by gently prizing off the seal, taking out the old cork and replacing it with a new one. He approached a few but to no avail, so he asked me to fly over and do it for him. He gave me all the details so that I could find someone to make a new cork, but before I could organize the flight, he called me back with some dire news.

Black had left the bottle standing upright in a closet, thinking it would be safe there, and departed on a tour. His father-in-law, who was keeping an eye on the house, walked into the closet and accidentally knocked the bottle over. Imagine: liquid gold flooring! Both of us are still grieving over the loss of this precious cognac. The worst thing was that neither of us had tasted one drop! Even now, I feel weak at the memory it.

WHAT IS A VINTAGE COGNAC?

A vintage cognac is made from the grape harvest of a single year, distilled and poured into a cask to mature. When the cellar-master considers that the cognac has reached maturity, it is moved from the cask into a glass demijohn, where it remains until it is bottled. Some cognac may go directly into a bottle. The year on the label is the year the cognac was harvested, distilled and put into the cask; it has nothing to do with when the spirit was bottled. Cognac does not age in bottle, and therefore it can be kept for over 100 years or more. Remember that a vintage could only be declared by a house up until 1963 (*see* Chapter 7).

A vintage cognac is quite unlike vintage wines, which, while they are labelled with the year of the harvest (the vintage), can continue to age in bottle. In addition, the life of some wine can be short by comparison; after a few years, for example, some white wines lose their freshness and quality, although red wine can last much longer, depending on its robustness.

With champagne and port, a vintage is declared when the harvest has taken place in an exceptional year, and not every year is declared a vintage.

Today, only a select few houses are allowed to declare vintage cognacs, including A E Dor, Delamain and Hine. Their bonded *chais* can be only opened in the presence of someone from the BNIC. All stock locked in the bonded *chai* has a genuine cellar record: when it was distilled, when it was put in cask, etc. This way, the BNIC protects consumers from any fraudulent practices.

TASTING PRE-PHYLLOXERA COGNACS

There is an intriguing difference between tasting a pre-phylloxera cognac (pre-1872/73) and a recent vintage cognac. Pre-phylloxera cognacs were made, for the most part, with Folle Blanche grapes. Only five per cent of the cognac region is planted with Folle Blanche today because it yields less per hectare and is, according to some, a capricious vine, difficult to grow and to harvest.

To me, Folle Blanche yields the finest floral bouquet with the longest, most rounded finish after a longer ageing process. Every time I open a bottle from the pre-phylloxera era, it has a richer, deeper colour, and is less leathery – something that I do not usually find when I open a more recent cognac.

Maurice Hennessy puts it this way: 'Sure, the taste was different, and not only because of the different type of rootstock. In those days, cognac was also distilled in a different way; the process was more difficult and not as precise as now, the vinification not as good. Distillation then was a question of a distiller and the talent of an oven-master. You had to know how to handle an oven heated by coal or wood, and it was hard to moderate the temperature. Now it is all gas-heated, so it is easy. These days, the emphasis is on the

palate: you need a good taster and you train the guy to be a good taster; it's easier to find a taster than to find a guy who has to taste *and* handle a fire. Plus we have better machinery. The quality of the wines is better for all these reasons.'

KEY POINTS OF VINTAGE COGNAC

During a visit to Courvoisier's *paradis*, I saw rows of old casks placed along each wall, dating from different centuries. The year was clearly written in chalk on each cask. Yet there were only a few old bottles placed on shelves in deep shadow. There is a mystique about old bottles that contain vintage cognac.

To read the story behind a bottle and its label, it is necessary to be a detective, looking for clues all the while. When I inspect a vintage cognac, I look to see if there is a lead or concrete cap around the bottle's neck; then I look for the stamped seal and a definition of the vintage date. Depending upon the year, I check to see that the bottle is the correct shape for the period, since there are specific years when the shapes changed from squat to cylindrical. Often, there will be a difference between the age of the bottle and the age of its contents, a situation verified by experts at Christie's of London, who also examine bottles of vintage cognac regularly.

P200/1: THE EYE CAN TELL YOU A LOT FROM A STEADY GAZE. HERE, AN EXPERIENCED CELLARMAN APPLIES HIS VISUAL JUDGEMENT TO A COGNAC SAMPLE.

Very early bottles from the 1700s and 1800s are usually hand-blown. If they aren't, then I would be suspicious, since machine-made bottles belong to a later period. The glass of hand-blown bottles will have many imperfections, such as air bubbles or a longish vein running through a part of the glass. These add character to the bottle, as well as reassure you that they are genuinely old.

Around 1811, with the advent of mechanical moulding for wine and spirit bottles, the art of glassblowing began to decline. Bottle shapes began to alter when the manufacturing process changed from hand-blown to machine-moulded. Slowly the bottles progressed from being slightly squat to more cylindrical, with a longer, elegant neck.

Apart from the pure mechanics of bottling, would-be connoiseurs should be aware of two additional aspects of vintage cognac bottles. They are is either bottled in France, or else they are what is called 'Early Landed', which means that they were bottled in Bristol, Birmingham or London in England.

FRENCH-BOTTLED COGNAC

Before 1857, most houses in Cognac or Jarnac either exported their cognac in cask, or bottled it in France for sale to a wealthy merchant, a noble customer or a chic restaurant, such as Maxim's of Paris. Some of the early French bottles (late 1700s and early 1800s) featured handwritten labels, which occasionally included the name of the house and a stamped seal.

These early cylindrical bottles also have a lead or a type of concrete protective cap around the neck. The turquoise or bluish glass is light in weight and colour; there are bubbles in the glass as well as other small marks that signify impurities. The 'kick-up', another term for the dimple in the base, also reveals the bottle's handmade origins, since it is not of a regular form.

In contrast, a typical French cognac bottle of the early 20th century would be of a two-piece, spun-mould construction, be of a pale aquamarine green colour, and feature a stamped seal. Some of these stamped seals are intricately designed; others are merely the year stamped in the glass.

EARLY LANDED COGNAC

Cognac that was exported in cask to England was kept in a bonded warehouse in Bristol, Birmingham or London, sometimes for decades, and then bottled by the wine and spirit merchant that purchased it. These individuals and companies included Avery's or John Harvey & Sons of Bristol, Harry Butler & Sons or Oldfields of York, and Justerini & Brooks or Berry Brothers & Rudd of St James' in London (the latter are located in an extraordinary ancient building which features interesting displays of both new and vintage bottles, and various assorted equipment associated with wine and spirits.

On labels of early landed cognac bottled around the 1870s, only the name of the shipper is printed, as well as the date the firm was established and the type of cognac the bottle contains, such as Grande Fine Champagne. Occasionally, the label will also mention the name of the house from whence the cognac originated, but not always.

OPPOSITE: A HANDMADE BOTTLE IS UNIQUE, OFTEN WITH SMALL DEFECTS IN THE GLASS, YET EACH HAS ITS OWN TRUE ELEGANCE.

A SHORT HISTORY OF BOTTLE-MAKING

From the middle of the 17th century, European and English bottles became integrated due to trade between the two regions. It is thought that the English were inspired by the French style of shaft-and-globe bottle, which had been in production before their English counterparts. Sealing bottles became common in the 1630s. Many European bottles of the 17th and 18th century were made with a narrow, cone-shaped kick-up; French mould-formed bottles in the 18th century feature a deep kick-up. Early moulds were tapered at one end to make the removal of the finished bottle easier.

Interestingly, Bristol was second only to London as a major glassmaking area for the United Kingdom. In 1725, some 15 glass houses were in business there – more, in fact, than in the capital. In 1770, British taxes on bottle glass were levied according to weight.

During the 19th century, the emphasis focused on moulding in order to regulate shape, which, in its way, regulated capacity. Some mould-formed bottles were produced in Bristol in 1811, by a firm called Henry Ricketts. By 1821, Ricketts had been granted a patent for his three-piece mould. And in 1845 the duty payable on glass bottles was dropped altogether.

Many of the cognac bottles I have bought are similar in shape to those made in the period between 1850 to 1900 – that is, they are moulded bottles in a narrow, cylindrical form, featuring a shallow kick-up in the base, and a stamped seal. Seals enjoyed a renaissance during the latter part of the 19th century, when wine and liquor merchants re-adopted the habit mainly as a way of promoting their wares.

OPPOSITE: LABELS WERE FIRST SEEN IN THE 17TH CENTURY BUT IT WAS NOT UNTIL THE 19TH CENTURY THAT TRADEMARKS BEGAN TO APPEAR ON LABELS.

In modern marketing terminology, this stamped seal would be called a 'logo', since it signified a brand.

There are some fascinating specialist books on the subject of the history of glassware and bottle-making and if you wish to learn more, I suggest you while away a few hours in the antiques section of a good book store. Auction houses in your area may also be helfpul with advice on good reference material.

1844
HINE & Cº
ESTABLISHED 1763
COGNAC
FINE CHAMPAGNE

SEGUIN
MOREAU

VINTAGE NOTES

1800
BIGNON GRANDE CHAMPAGNE

This bottle has a decorative label, but the information on it is sparse. However, it is a pressed bottle, like the shape of an 1860 or 1870, with imperfections and a slight 'kick-up' in the base.

Tasting note:
Shows a rich, amber colour. The aroma is intense, with a sweet note of spices and flowers. On the palate, there is a pleasant taste of sweet almonds and an elegant, long aftertaste.

THE YEAR IN HISTORY:
Federal government moves to Washington DC in the United States. Napoléon conquers Italy. Alessandro Volta produces electricity.

P208/9: THE STAMP OF SEGUIN MOREAU – THE LARGEST COOPERAGE IN FRANCE

1804
MASSOUGES

An imperial half-gallon bottle. Hand-made half-gallons are an unusual size, and the bottle probably was made much earlier and kept for special cognacs such as this. The cognac itself was taken out of the cask around 1860. The label is interesting, since before the mid-1850s, all cognacs had to be sold for blending, and no house labels were made. This particular label dates from around 1865 and represents one of the earliest printed.

Tasting note:
Offers a straw, slightly grey-gold colour. The aroma contains a surprisingly high level of vanilla, but also some vine, cane and leather notes. The flavour is lively, though dry, but with a *rancio*, floral and straw taste, and hazelnut and oak nuances.

THE YEAR IN HISTORY:
Napoléon crowns himself Emperor of France. Lewis and Clarke begin exploration of what is now the American northwest.

1805
FINE CHAMPAGNE DE L'EMPEREUR

This interesting dark-green bottle has a wax cap around its neck. The label reads 'Réserve de Sazarac de Forge & Fils, plus Maison Fondée en 1782', and a separate oval label bears the date 1805. This bottle has probably been kept in cellar and labelled by the house much later. It features a seal with the capital letter 'N' surrounded by a Roman laurel leaf.

Tasting note:
The colour of deep amber, it offers a voluptuous, multi-layered aroma of warm, ripe fruit with a hint of mushroom and wood. The palate is smooth, with vanilla-tinged fruit. Waves of aftertastes reveal new flavours – an incredibly rich texture for such an old cognac.

THE YEAR IN HISTORY:
French and Spanish fleets defeated by Admiral Nelson at Trafalgar; Nelson mortally wounded. Napoléon defeats Austrian and Russian forces at the Battle of Austerlitz; crowns himself King of Italy.

GRANDE CHAMPAGNE
1800

VIEILLES EAUX DE VIE FINES
DE
COGNAC
MEDAILLE D'OR
J.B.E. DE MASSOUGNES
Propriétaire
Aux Fontaines près Cognac
par AIGRE-CHARENTE
Récolte de 1800

DE L'EMPEREUR
1805

1809
COGNAC

This burgundy-style bottle is pale green with a deep 'kick-up' in the base. There is a stamped seal with the date '1809' below the neck.

Tasting note:
This cognac is a deep-gold colour, with interesting reflections. On the nose, there is a scent of herbs and flowers (rose and violet) along with a hint of damp wood. It is round on the palate – almost oily, with a woody note. It boasts a definite masculine aroma and a full body, developing a delicious strength on the aftertaste.

THE YEAR IN HISTORY:
Rome added to the French Empire; Pope Pious VII ex-communicates Napoléon; Pope imprisoned at Savona. Britain's Dartmoor Prison opens for business.

1815
FROMY GRANDE FINE CHAMPAGNE

This small, pale-green, pressed bottle dates from the early 1900s and states the name of the cognac house and the year it was distilled.

Tasting note:
Shows a warm, amber colour, with distinct floral notes of carnation and rose on the nose. On the palate, flavours include ripe fruit and spices, vanilla and licorice. It is also buttery and nutty, with a trace of *rancio*, and ends in a warm, elegant aftertaste, but has a short finish.

THE YEAR IN HISTORY:
The Battle of Waterloo: the French defeated by Duke of Wellington; Napoléon tries to escape but fails and surrenders; he is banished to island of St Helena.

1824
COURVOISIER & CURLIER FRERES GRANDE FINE CHAMPAGNE

This pale-green bottle shows a deep 'kick-up' in the base, with a printed label revealing the eagle logo combined with a crown. It has a red wax cap. I would guess that the cognac was bottled in the early 1900s.

Tasting note:
Boasts a dark colour with orange reflections. The aroma is elegant, offering notes of rum, almonds and a soft hint of spice. On the palate, there is a distinct flavour of plum and hints of almond, all rounded off in a long, rich aftertaste.

THE YEAR IN HISTORY:
Beethoven's Ninth Symphony performed. Louis XVIII dies and Charles X ascends French throne. Lord Byron dies. Imperial gallon established as a standard liquid measure.

1809

1815
FONDÉE EN 1815
Grande Fine Champag
Fromy
COGNAC
1815

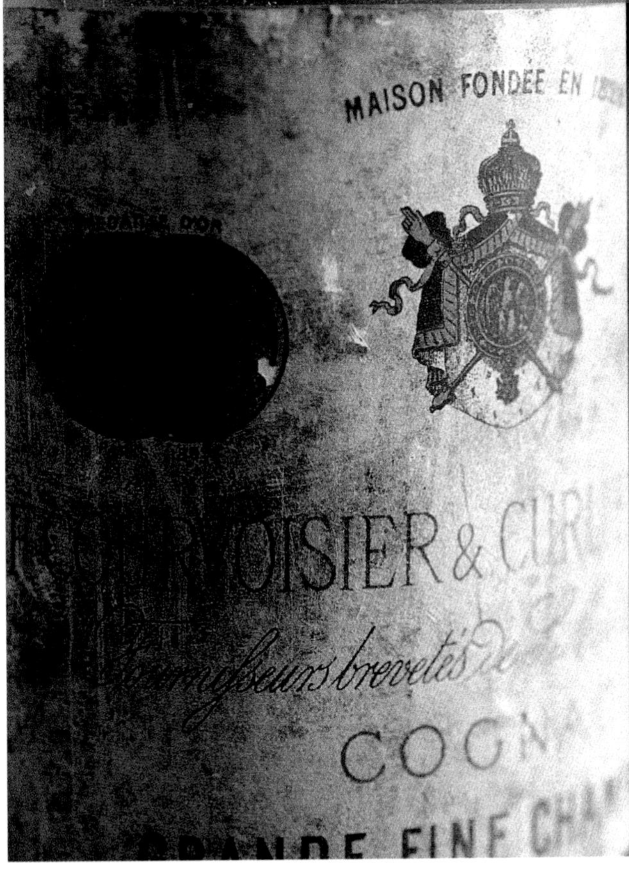
MAISON FONDÉE EN
OISIER & CU
brevetés
COG
GRANDE FINE CHA

1830
CAMUS RESERVE GRANDE CHAMPAGNE COGNAC 'LA GRANDE MARQUE'

The moulded bottle is a delicate pale-green with no 'kick-up' in the base. It bears the Camus *croix* stamped on the lower neck. Stamped just below the neck at the back of the bottle are the words *Grande Marque.*

Tasting note:
A dark, amber-coloured cognac with a wonderful aroma of dried fruit (sweet raisins and plums), cinnamon and nutmeg. It is complex, full of the taste of honey, spices, chocolate, and a touch of woody mushrooms, with an endless aftertaste.

THE YEAR IN HISTORY:
Charles X forced to abdicate; Louis Philippe, 'The Citizen King', rules France. The Royal Geographical Society is founded in England.

PP214/5: THE IMPRESSIVE WAREHOUSE (THE BLACKENED END) AND THE OFFICES (LESS BLACKENED) BELONGING TO THE HOUSE OF TIFFON ON THE BANKS OF THE RIVER CHARENTE AT JARNAC.

1848
A DE LUZE & FILS GRAND COGNAC FINE CHAMPAGNE

This dark-green moulded bottle has a long neck and, interestingly, no 'kick-up'. The cognac was probably put into the bottle around 1910.

Tasting note:
Shows a beautiful, deep-mahogany colour with a fiery-red reflection. The aroma is hearty, rich and fruity. The palate is complex and almost temperamental on the tongue, bitter and vibrant, but with a pleasant spicy aftertaste.

THE YEAR IN HISTORY:
Revolution throughout Europe. End of United States and Mexican War; Mexico cedes claims to Texas, California, Arizona, Utah, New Mexico and Nevada. Karl Marx and Friedrich Engels publish The Communist Manifesto.

1864
J G MONNET LA SALAMANDRE

A fire-breathing dragon heralds this cognac. The bottle is tall and elegant, pale-turquoise in colour, handmade with imperfections and boasting a lead seal. The cognac was probably put into the bottle in the early 1900s.

Tasting note:
Complex stuff: chestnut in colour with a huge, spicy aroma, and a deep note of oak. The long, warm finish has a hint of vanilla, molasses, leather and a touch of pepper. On the palate, there is a sweetness of raisins followed by a lingering chocolate aftertaste.

THE YEAR IN HISTORY:
In the United States, the Civil War continues: Ulysses S Grant is made commander-in-chief of Union forces; Sherman marches Union troops through Georgia, burning Atlanta to the ground. Charles Dickens publishes Our Mutual Friend. *Henrik Ibsen writes* The Pretenders.

RÉSERVE 1830
GRANDE CHAMPAGNE
LA GRANDE

A. DE LUZE & FILS
GRAND
COGNAC FINE CHAMPAGNE
1848

J.G MONNET
SALAMANDRE
VINICOLES

1865
BOUTILLIER, G BRIAND & CO COGNAC

This pale-green, moulded bottle features the words 'Trade Mark' accompanied by a logo featuring an atlas of the world overprinted with Cognac, supported by a small group of cherubs and what appear to be two lions. I think the cognac was bottled in the early 1900s.

Tasting note:
This is a classic vintage cognac, sporting a deep, warm colour with red-brick tones. It has the aroma of cigars, woody mushrooms, and some delicate, floral notes. On the tongue, it has a pleasant *rancio* taste which continues to expand. There's a hint of sweetness and nutty vanilla on the after-taste – truly superb.

THE YEAR IN HISTORY:
United States Civil War ends; President Abraham Lincoln assassinated. Joseph Lister performs first antiseptic surgery. Lewis Carroll's Alice's Adventures in Wonderland *published. Count Leo Tolstoy's* War and Peace *published.*

1872
MARTELL

A fascinating early, pale-green, moulded bottle of Martell Early Landed cognac that features a lead cap embossed with the name of the importer. Quite a few imperfections in the glass, and there is no 'kick-up' in the base. The label is simple, stating 'Martell's 1872 Guaranteed Genuine as Imported' and 'Bottled by Henry Mitchell & Co, Limited, Cape Hill, Birmingham.'

Tasting note:
Shows a rich, golden-brown colour. The winey, raisiny nose offers a hint of mushrooms. It is soft and elegant on the tongue, with delicately unfolding secondary flavours of vanilla; a long, clean aftertaste rounds it off.

THE YEAR IN HISTORY:
Ulysses S Grant re-elected President of the United States. In Britain, the Licensing Act decrees that public houses should close at midnight in London and at 10PM in the country. Penny-farthing bicycle in general use in London. Jules Verne's Around the World in 80 Days *published.*

1914
CROIZET GRANDE RÉSERVE VINTAGE COGNAC

This is one of the first bottles with a label stating the proof and volume of liquid inside: 'contains not less than 24 fl oz of 70° proof cognac'. A dark-green, moulded bottle with a 'kick-up' in the base, its label also states the name of the house. It has a wax cap, and I would venture to say that the cognac was probably put into the bottle before the Second World War.

Tasting note:
The colour of antique gold. The aroma is lively, with notes of sweet orange, walnut and a hint of cinnamon and floral tones. On the palate, there is a hint of spice, combined with a nutty, vanilla-and-toffee richness. A lingering, nutty finish completes the picture.

THE YEAR IN HISTORY:
First World War begins with the assassination of Archduke Franz Ferdinand at Sarajevo. In Cognac, this becomes 'The Year of the Lady'. First of the Tarzan *books, by Edgar Rice Burroughs, published.*

TRADE
COGNAC

FINEST LIQUEUR COGNAC BRANDY
MARTELL'S 1872
GUARANTEED GENUINE AS IMPORTED
Bottled by
HENRY MITCHELL & CO., Limited,
Cape Hill,

GRANDE
VINTAGE 1914
70° PROOF NOT LESS THAN 24
B.L. Croizet-Cognac
PRODUCE OF FRANCE
Established

Grand
Fine
Champagne
1875

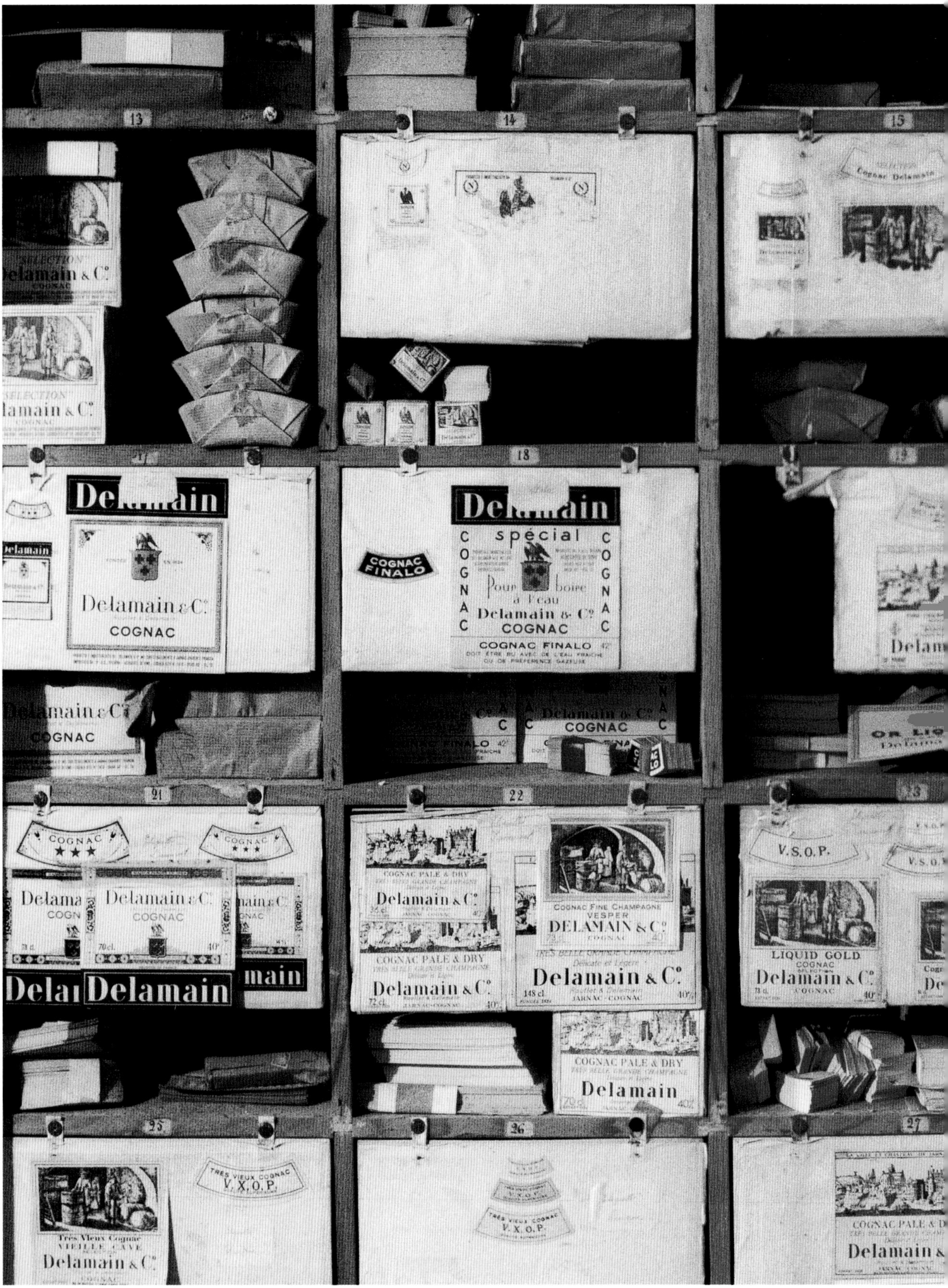
13
14
15
SELECTION
Delamain & Cº
COGNAC
Delamain & Cº
COGNAC
18
spécial
COGNAC FINALO
Pour boire à l'eau
Delamain & Cº
COGNAC
COGNAC FINALO 42°
DOIT ÊTRE BU AVEC DE L'EAU FRAICHE OU DE PRÉFÉRENCE GAZEUSE
21
22
COGNAC ★★★
Delamain & Cº
COGNAC
70 cl.
40°
Delamain
COGNAC PALE & DRY
Delamain & Cº
COGNAC FINE CHAMPAGNE
VESPER
DELAMAIN & Cº
COGNAC
Délicate et Légère
Delamain & Cº
148 cl.
JARNAC-COGNAC
V.S.O.P.
LIQUID GOLD
COGNAC
Delamain & Cº
COGNAC
Delamain
25
26
27
TRÈS VIEUX COGNAC
V.X.O.P.
Très Vieux Cognac
VIEILLE CAVE
Delamain & Cº

A FEW GOOD NAMES

'Cognac has all the medicinal virtues of alcohol consumed in small quantities.... It is therefore comparable to food, a food that brings you calories and strength.'

ROBERT DELAMAIN

ON THE FOLLOWING PAGES YOU WILL FIND A PERSONAL SELECTION OF JUST 30 COGNAC HOUSES CHOSEN FOR THEIR UNIQUENESS, be they a 'boutique' house or a multinational conglomerate. I have written about only a few of their cognac styles, ranging from a VSOP to a Family Reserve (usually, their finest blends from the ancient stocks held in their respective paradis).

P220/1: DELAMAIN HAS A WONDERFUL COLLECTION OF LABELS DATING BACK TO THE 1950S IN A CUPBOARD IN THE FAMILY HOUSE.

These are just a small proportion of the 250 cognac houses that operate throughout the region. This book is about my own exploration of cognac, and these are the houses I have encountered on my tasting journey. They represent every *cru* in the region, from Grande Champagne to Bons Bois, and their products are available in most world markets. Some of the brands are immediately recognizable; others are strangers that you will want to get to know. There is enough variety in the types here that I am sure you will find one to satisfy your palate.

The fact that I have not written about the remaining 220 houses is in no way a reflection upon the quality of their products. I love *all* cognac. Yet, space is at a premium in a book such as this, and I had to some make tough decisions. So, if I have left out any particular favourites, please forgive me.

A DE FUSSIGNY

Established in Jarnac in 1987 by Alain and Anne-Marie Royer. Anne-Marie is a descendant of wine-grower and explorer Antoine de Fussigny, and her husband is Alain Louis, of the Royer dynasty. Both are committed to producing authentic cognacs, full of flavour and style.

VSOP Special Ebony Blend
Made with a high proportion of Grand and Petite Champagne *eau-de-vie*. The colour is dark brown, with touches of red. The nose shows port and mature sherry hints, followed by red fruit, liquorice, and curry tones mixed with dark chocolate. The palate is velvety, and dense, with touches of toasted coffee. The finish is long.

Cognac XO
A blend of Grande Champagne, Petite Champagne and Fins Bois, with a dominance of Grande Champagne. A deep, golden-yellow cognac, with delicate fragrances of jasmine, honeysuckle, young port, fresh walnuts, spices, ginger and dried fruit. On the palate, there is a concentration of balanced, mellow flavours. A long finish rounds it off.

Très Vieille Grande Champagne
50 years old
Deep-yellow, with fiery mahogany and red tones. The nose offers many fragrances: a floral note of jasmine, port, spices, dried fruits, old oak and saffron touches. Concentrated, with a long, lasting finish.

A E DOR

A small prestigious house known for the superb old cognacs hidden deep in its *paradis*. There are 11 different styles, ranging from Cognac Sélection at five years old to a Vieille Réserve No 11 at 70 years old. The latest product is an XO decanter designed for the Scandinavian and the duty-free markets. Odile and Jacques Rivière, descendants of founder Amédée-Edouard Dor, have been directors of the company since 1981.

Rare Fine Champagne
8 years old
A blend of equal parts of Grand and Petite Champagne *eaux-de-vie*, aged in oak to give it a fine amber colour. The nose is warm and generous, with floral tones. A long-lasting finish ends a palate showing plenty of finesse.

Cigar Reserve
Created in 1966 for the German and American markets. A blend of old Grand and Petite Champagne, aged in new oak, contrary to tradition. The nose shows spice and a woody, tobacco hint. The palate is very smooth, with a long finish revealing a lot of vanilla and an aggressive note to balance the cigar-like flavours.

Vieille Réserve No 11
Over 70 years old
This is blended by Odile Rivière exclusively from Grande Champagne *eaux-de-vie* (some are pre-phylloxera). Light, bright mahogany, with a hint of *rancio* and mature plums on the nose. The palate is round and soft, offering a taste of chocolate before a long-lasting finish.

BISQUIT

Founded in Jarnac in 1819 by Alexandre Bisquit, a salt-trader who became Mayor of Cognac after the Revolution in 1848. Bisquit's Domaine de Lignères is the largest vineyard in the region, with 64 copper stills, its own cooperage and a bottling plant on site. The house is known for the fruity richness of its young cognacs. In 1965 the family sold the company to Paul Ricard. At the prestigious 2000 Paris Agricultural Show, Bisquit's VSOP Fine Champagne was awarded a gold medal.

VSOP Fine Champagne
7 to 8 years old
This cognac sports the colour of old gold, showing subtle overtones of wood, flowers and spices on the nose, which flow over onto the palate, where they become more intense. A lingering finish completes a very satisfying picture indeed.

Château de Lignères
Aged for a minimum of 10 years
A pure, single-estate cognac from the Domaine de Lignères. Distinctive stuff, with an amber colour, and a subtle, rounded bouquet with hints of almonds, walnuts, dried apricot and honey. Vine and lime-blossom flavours continue on the palate, which offers a taste of honey on the finish.

Cohiba Cognac Extra
40 to 50 years old
This is a blend of 90 per cent Ugni Blanc and 10 per cent Colombard and Folle Blanche grapes from Grande Champagne. Deep amber and mahogany in colour, it boasts scents of candied fruit and wildflowers on the nose, with hints of fresh wood. The palate has a velvety texture, with honey and toffee notes and a persistent, spicy finish. Presented in a crystal decanter in a stylish wooden box.

OPPOSITE: DRYING BOTTLES ON THE SLANT IS A QUICK, EASY AND CREATIVE METHOD IN USE AT A E DOR.

CAMUS

One of the top six cognac companies, founded by wine-grower Jean-Baptiste Camus in 1863. The basis for its *assemblages* are *eaux-de-vies* from four family estates: Château d'Uffaut and Château Bonneuil in Grande Champagne, and Château du Plessis and Château Vignolles in the Borderies regions. This supplies only a small percentage of the requirements so current president Jean-Paul Camus buys aged distillates from about 250 vintners. He acts as his own cellar-master, blending up to 170 different *eaux-de-vie* of different vintages to make just one cognac.

Camus Grand VSOP
A blend of five *crus*, it is deep gold, with a touch of fire. The fragrant, fruity nose is enhanced by hints of fresh flowers (violets, hyacinths). The palate is full-bodied and aromatic, with a neat, fresh-fruit flavour associated with delicate touches of chestnut and spices. Finishes long and clean.

Camus XO Superior
Deep gold to mahogany in colour, though very bright and showing a limpid quality. The nose offers plenty of fruity, woody aromas married with the delicate scents of prunes and flowers. The palate is mellow, bursting with the richness of full-bodied fruit enhanced by a nutty *rancio* character. A fragrant finish rounds it off superbly.

Jubilee
Released to celebrate the 50th anniversary of the present company, Jubilee is a blend of special stocks from five main growths. It is deep amber in colour, with shades of mahogany. On the nose, you find sandalwood, vanilla and cigar box are enhanced by hints of violet and irises. On the palate, flavours range from crystallized orange to wood undertones. An exceptional finish with violet and pepper hints make this appropriate for any anniversary.

DOMINIQUE CHANIER & FILS

Members of the Chanier family are known as producers of Pineau des Charentes (a regional fortified wine drunk as an aperitif) as well as cognac. In 1985, Dominique Chanier took over the family's vineyards at Arthenac and began to expand the retail trade under his name.

In 1988, he and his wife Nicole purchased 18 hectares in Lignières Sonneville, in the Grande Champagne region. Both vineyards are planted with Ugni Blanc, but at Arthenac, Colombard and Merlot have also been planted. Every stage of winemaking and cognac production is handled on site, making this a true 'boutique' house.

VSOP
5 to 8 years old
A blend of Petit Champagne cognacs. It has a clear, gold colour, while on the nose there are fruity aromas of pears and green peppers. The palate offers a light body, and the finish is sweet. Very good as part of a long drink.

Très Vieille Réserve
25 years old
Made exclusively with Petite Champagne, this is the oldest of the range. The nose is spicy with a note of cocoa. The palate is soft and fine: well-balanced with a delicate finish.

COURVOISIER

Proud of its heritage as the official supplier to the imperial court of Napoléon III, this Jarnac-based company is challenging the white-spirit drinker to trade up and try some of its cognac.

Napoléon
A blend of Grande and Petite Champagne ranging from 15 to 25 years old. The colour is deep-gold to amber, and it offers an aroma of cigar boxes, with touches of prune, liquorice, hazelnut, port, gingerbread and orange-blossom. Full-bodied, mellow and round on the palate, it boasts cigar and woody notes and a long, intense finish.

XO Impérial
A blend of Grande and Petite Champagne with a small quantity of very old Borderies cognacs. Shows an exotic bouquet of vanilla, cocoa and amber on the nose, while the palate offers surprising complexity and finesse. The finish is smooth and seductive.

L'Esprit de Courvoisier
Younger cognacs in this blend date back to 1930, while others are from the 19th century and were used to supply the courts of Napoléon III and Edward VII of England. Elegant stuff, coloured a light amber-gold. The nose is rich and vibrant, with hints of port, roasted coffee beans, hot fruit cake, cinnamon and honey. The palate is full-bodied, revealing a velvety smoothness. Finishes long and mellow.

Initial Extra
An unusual blend of 35- to 100-year-old Grande Champagne and Borderies *eaux-de-vie*, this deep, golden-yellow cognac has a rich, complex nose offering notes of truffles, port, cigars, prunes, cedar, cinnamon, dried apricots, crystallized oranges, irises and violets. The palate is deep, harmonious and elegant, full of delicacy. The extremely long finish varies from mushrooms to a subtle hint of cigar leaves, ending with spice notes.

P226/7: JEAN-PAUL CAMUS AND HIS NOSE AT WORK DECIDING WHICH COGNAC WILL BE USED WITH OTHERS IN A FINAL BLEND FOR ONE OF CAMUS' COGNACS.

CROIZET

Located in Saint-Même-les-Carrières in the heart of Grande Champagne. In 1805, Léon Croizet began to sell cognac and was awarded the Legion of Honor for his work against phylloxera. The family estates are planted with 430,000 vines producing up to 1.6 million litres of white wine for the company's Grande Champagne stocks; it also buys and distils Petite Champagne, Borderies and Fins Bois to add to them.

Croizet concentrates on older and rarer cognacs, such as XO and single vintages. Currently, Philippe Eymard, a charming international ambassador for cognac, is president of the company, and his two sons, François and Bertrand, are moving the business forward.

VSOP
Coloured a deep amber, this is a blend of Grande and Petite Champagne, Fins Bois and Bons Bois *eaux-de-vie*. On the nose, there are pleasant notes of flowers (roses, irises) and citrus fruits. The palate is light, revealing a hint of vanilla on the long finish.

XO Grande Champagne
30 years old
A deep, gold-coloured cognac, with some attractive vanilla and floral aromas on the nose. On the palate, there are hints of intense citrus fruits, along with walnut and vanilla flavours and a powerful, dry richness. The finish is long-lasting and elegant, with a grapefruity dryness.

DANIEL BOUJU

Cognacs from this artisan house, founded in 1805 in the heart of Grande Champagne at Saint-Preuil, are characterized by the finesse of their bouquets and a rich taste. The cognacs range in age from five to 40 years old.

Royal
15 years old
A smooth, chestnut-coloured, unfiltered cognac, 60 per cent abv. Long on the finish, with complex aromas that go well with a cigar.

XO No 27
27 years old
From Grande Champagne grapes aged in new Limousin oak casks; 42.7 per cent abv. Amber; strong and subtle on the nose, with hints of spice, vanilla, prunes and *rancio* touches adding to the palate's remarkable length.

Réserve Familiale
80 years old
Made from Ugni Blanc, Colombard and Folle Blanche Grande Champagne grapes. In this unfiltered cognac, the *rancio* Charentais flavour is increasingly complex and enriched by fruity notes. An exceptional length on the palate makes it a good addition to anyone's collection.

Diabolo Cognac
·ALBERT JARRAUD·COGNAC·
DÉPOSÉ

TRADE MARK
VSO
EXTRA SUPÉRIEUR
1850
COMANDON & Co
COGNAC
Maison Fondée en
1821
LONDON OFFICES 74, Great Tower St
E. P. GAUDRY
DEPOSITARIO Y APODERADO – APARTADO 2247 – TELÉFONO 1598
MÉXICO

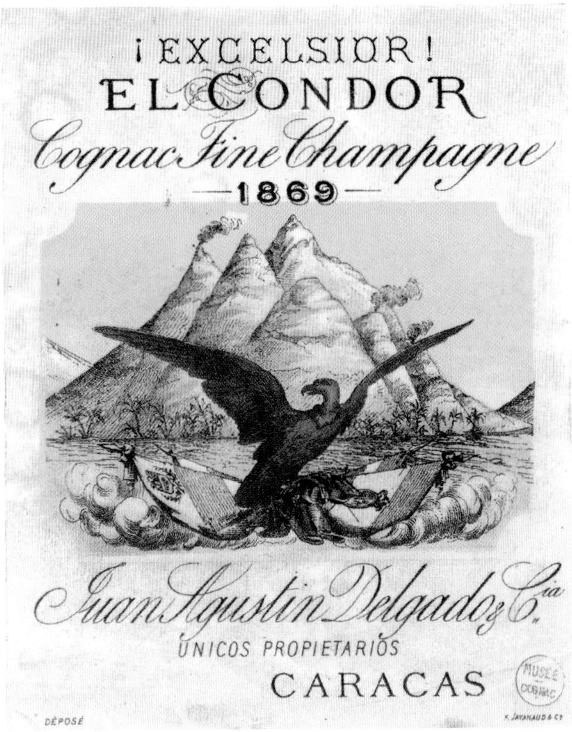

PP230/1: COLOUR, DESIGN AND CREATIVITY ARE ABUNDANT IN THIS SELECTION OF LABELS FROM THE 19TH CENTURY.

DELAMAIN

One of the most select cognac houses, Delamain is located in Jarnac. In 1824, the house was established by Henry Delamain with a Roullet cousin. In 1920, Delamain became the sole owner. The house maintains a tradition of craftsmanship that sets perfection above commercial priority. The firm produces only Grande Champagne cognac. It does not own vineyards and does not distil, preferring to buy in its stocks and blend on the premises.

Pale and Dry XO
Grande Champagne Cognac
20 to 25 years old

This cognac represents 80 per cent of Delamain's total output and was developed in the 1920s. Its colour is a bright, velvety gold. The palate acquires an intense fruitiness, accompanied by floral hints. There is also a lingering aftertaste of vanilla, subtly laced with liquorice.

Vesper Grande Champagne Cognac

Created in the 1950s, Vesper is 100 per cent Grande Champagne, and uses, on average, cognacs that are 10 years older than those used for Pale and Dry. It offers an amber hue, with a glint of pure gold. Its suave bouquet reveals its complexity: a hint of oak gives way to scents of wood, dry vine shoots, vanilla and sunburned grape pips. On the palate, it is mellow, with a lingering finish.

Très Venerable Grande Champagne Cognac
45 to 55 years old

The oldest in Delamain's range. Its colour is amber-topaz, and its effect is sensual. Aromas blossom into an unexpectedly refreshing sensation, subtly evocative of liquorice, that lingers in the mouth. The maturity of the nose conceals an apparent lightness; the intense liveliness of its 'bite' leaves only a lingering, velvety caress.

PHILIPPE BRAASTAD-TIFFON

After 20 years with the family firm, Tiffon (*see* page 251), differing opinions led to Philippe Braastad-Tiffon's departure and this new venture. His philosophy is summed up by the motto: 'Great Quality Cognac in a Cask'. Based on the quayside of the Charente at Jarnac, this is a small but high-quality new venture worth including – despite the fact that it currently produces just 6,000 bottles each year and sells only to Finland and England.

Duquai XO
15 years old

The colour is reminiscent of a shining crystal, with a mid-tawny core and mid-ochre-to-green rim. Complex fruit and flower scents make up the nose, which also shows an elegant balance of wood gleaned from its Limousin and Tronçais casks. The palate is long, with a symphony of taste sensations reflecting its 15 years of age.

P234/5: MODERN DISTILLERIES ARE A FAR CRY FROM THE SMALLER, MORE RUSTIC ONES OF OLD.

PIERRE FERRAND

Founded in 1702, Pierre Ferrand's cellar in Ars contains cognacs distilled by his grandfather with grapes from the family's 75-hectare plot in the heart of Grande Champagne. Ferrand specializes in old cognacs: the youngest blend ages a minimum of 10 years before release. Distilled on the lees and unfiltered after fermentation, it retains subtle aromas of fruits and flowers. The house style is elegant, smooth and rich in layers and flavours. The *maître de chai* is Patrick Guidicelli, a Corsican. Ferrand also produces single-vineyard, single-vintage cognacs.

Réserve
20 years old
Winner of a bronze medal at the 2000 International Wine and Spirit Competition, Réserve boasts a fine gold colour. The nose shows scents of freshly picked grapes. Fruity and round, with a slight vanilla flavour on the palate, it ends with a subtle finish.

Sélection des Anges
30 years old
Named after the evaporation known as the 'angels' share', this cognac was commended in the 1999 International Wine and Spirit Competition for its old-gold colour, rich aroma and musky, spicy flavour. Its lingering finish offers rich, mellow flavours and hints of vanilla and liquorice.

Abel
45 years old
Sold in limited quantities, this old cognac is deep walnut in colour. Its initial aroma is of intense plums, raisins and cocoa with a hint of lemon zest, growing nuttier as time passes. Abel presents a huge body of flavour on its dry palate, which also boasts a hint of wildflowers. Long, with citrus-fruit notes and a hint of almonds.

FRAPIN

The Frapin family has a fascinating history. In the 17th century, Pierre Frapin served as apothecary to Louis XIV; the Frapin coat of arms was awarded in 1697 and appears on all of the Frapin Cognac bottles.

This exclusive business was founded in the 1800s by his descendant, also named Pierre. It produces only Grande Champagne cognacs from a single vineyard, its own, located in 300 hectares of the Domaine P Frapin in the *premier cru* region, near Segonzac. Since March 1997, the VIP XO Grande Champagne was the only cognac served on Concorde (until its flight suspension).

VSOP
A new release, this is the only 100 per cent Grande Champagne VSOP. It is a golden-amber colour, with a complex, grapey and floral bouquet. The palate derives its woody, vanilla touch from the tannin of the oak casks. Long-lasting, with good aromas and flavours on the finish.

XO Château Fontpinot
Winner of the 1998 International Spirits Challenge (XO Category) trophy and gold medal in London. The colour of warm gold, its nose is delicate and elegant, with woody

HENNESSY

fragrances giving way to floral tones and notes of vanilla, hawthorn and wildflowers. Very long-lasting flavours include crystallized apricots, oranges and port, as well as a *rancio* note on the finish.

Extra Patrimonial Réserve
40 to 50 years old
A blend of cognacs, Extra Patrimonial Reserve Pierre Frapin comes from the family reserve casks. Mahogany-coloured with hints of copper, it is a perfect balance of concentrated aromas, a smooth, complex and subtle blend of port mixed with scents of a wooden cigar boxes. Exceptionally long-lasting and subtle.

GAUTIER

The distillery has been situated in a water-mill at Aigre, in the heart of the Fins Bois region, since 1755, when Louis Gautier founded the company. The river runs beneath the cellars creating a constant high humidity – essential for ageing cognac. Gautier is holder of eight gold and silver medals from both the International Wine and Spirit Competition and the International Wine Competition of Vinexpo from 1990 to 2000. The XO won a gold medal at the International Wine and Spirit Competition in London, and the Tradition Rare was awarded a trophy.

Myriade
This is the second release in the company's Discovery Collection. It has a delicate, floral nose, and is smooth and round on the palate. It offers the characteristic flavours of dry fruit from the Grande Champagne *cru*, and shows a hint of hazelnut on its lengthy finish.

OPPOSITE: GAUTIER'S COGNAC BOTTLE REVEALS ITS CHARACTER IN ITS SHAPE AND ANTIQUITY.

Pinar del Rio Cigar Blend Cognac XO
Blended with cognacs dating back as far as the 1800s, Pinar del Rio gains body from the Fins Bois, mellowness from the Borderies and finesse and finish from the Petite and Grande Champagne grapes. Its colour is a rich amber, with mahogany and rosewood highlights. Rich on the nose, it has no aggressiveness, and offers fragrances of subtle vanilla, dried fruit and oak. On the palate, it is round and long, with finesse. The finish is well-balanced, and it gains increasing intensity without bite.

Tradition Rare
A 10th generation cognac and 43 per cent abv. This limited-edition release is mahogany in colour, with vanilla on the nose and persistent, rich aromas. Powerful, rich and full-bodied in flavour, it also offers mellow and velvety notes on the palate. Its excellent length magnifies the many levels of flavours before flowing into an exceptional finish.

CHAMPAGNE
FONDÉE EN
Guy

HARDY

In 1863, Antony Hardy moved to Cognac to control his supply of wines and spirits. Since then, five generations of Hardys have been born into the company. In 1945, Jacques Hardy travelled the world to sell Hardy's quality cognac; now his daughters Bénédicte and Sophie share this role. Patrick keeps an eye on the distillation of Grande and Petite Champagne, Fins Bois, and Borderies *eaux-de-vie*, while Jean-Antoine looks after the cellars.

VSOP Fine Champagne
Presented in a new, elegant bottle, this cognac has a burnished, luminous, copper colour. On the nose there is a hint of leather, lemon and pineapple. On the palate, hints of oak rub shoulders with vanilla and chocolate, all of which fade into a rounded finish that provides an almondy flavour.

Napoléon
12 to 15 years old
A blend of four *crus*: Grande and Petite Champagne, Borderies and Fins Bois. Coloured a mellow amber, it is delicate, elegant and smooth, with a lightly fruity aroma. The palate is well-structured, with rich flavours of nuts and honey. A polished finish rounds it off nicely.

XO
25 years old
A blend of Grande and Petite Champagne, with an amber-gold colour. It shows an elegant nose, with hints of apricot and roasted almonds. The palate's mouth-filling presence is soft, feminine, and boasts a rounded finish.

HENNESSY

The dominating company located on the quayside in Cognac, both the family and commercial history go back to 1765, when Richard Hennessy, an Irish immigrant and a French army officer, arrived in Cognac. Members of the Fillioux family, (currently it is Jann Fillioux), have served as *maître de chai* for the Hennessys for seven generations.

Pure White

Designed for a younger palate, Pure White is aged for three years in old oak casks. Light gold in colour, it reveals light floral notes with a powerful bouquet of fresh vines. On the palate it is fresh, which makes it good for mixing.

XO

Aged between 10 and 70 years

A dark, amber-coloured cognac with an intense, heavy, spicy aroma showing traces of dried prunes, wood and old leather. On the palate, dry fruit mixes with a hint of toffee and vanilla. Rich and masculine on the finish.

Paradis Extra

In 1873, Emile Fillioux blended this family-reserve cognac, laid it to rest in the cellar and asked the family not to use it until at least 100 years had passed. In 1979, Maurice Fillioux created Hennessy Paradis, and nephew Jann Fillioux, the seventh generation after Emile, created this one.

Released in 2001, this is a Fine cognac, and the oldest of the blend dates from 1870. The nose is complex, with a hint of pepper, and notes of flowers, cinnamon, crystallized fruit, truffles and honey. The palate is spicy at first, then shows a hint of *rancio*. Powerful stuff, with a long finish.

Richard Hennessy

A blend of the company's oldest *eaux-de-vie* from the *paradis*, it shows a deep, amber colour with a red core. On the nose, there is a hint of pepper and leather, followed by vanilla, spices and floral scents. The palate is smooth with a touch of spice, ripe fruit, oak and *rancio*. Persistent and harmonious to the end.

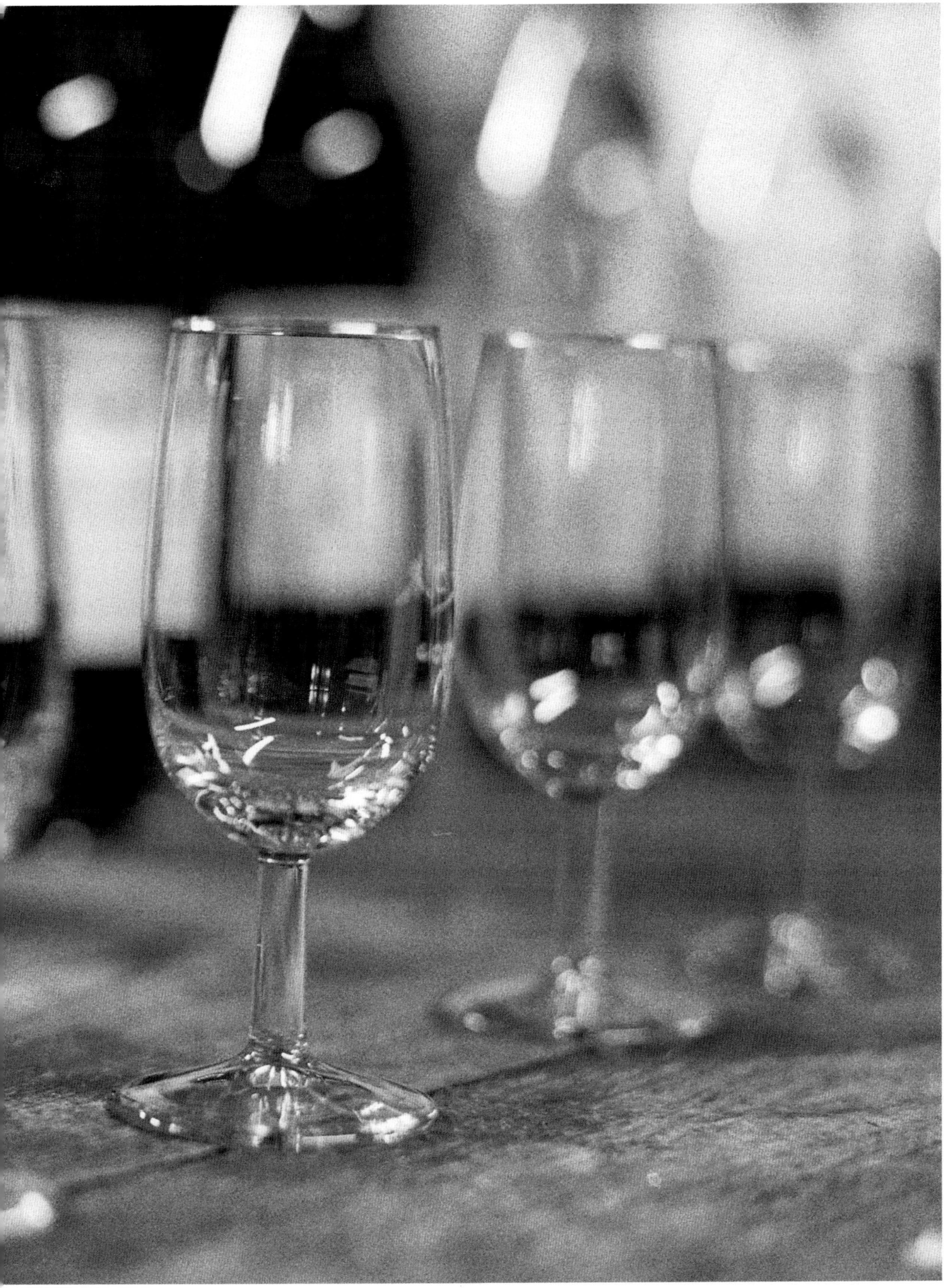

HINE

Formed when Thomas Hine came from his native Dorest to Jarnac to learn French. Since his death, his descendants have produced some of the world's finest cognacs blended from the best *crus* in the region: Grande and Petite Champagne. Bernard Hine is sixth generation and has the finest nose in Jarnac. Hine is one of the few firms registered to release vintage cognacs; the *paradis* holds a collection of aged cognacs awaiting bottling when the time is right. The house was granted a royal warrant as supplier of cognac to Her Majesty Queen Elizabeth II in 1962.

Rare and Delicate

After eight to 10 years of ageing – far longer than required at VSOP level – this blend of Grande and Petite Champagne has an exceptional bouquet and smoothness. Light amber in colour, on the nose finesse and elegance combine with the subtle floral aromas, while the palate is marked by a long, mellow finish.

Antique
20 to 25 years old

A Fine Champagne blend with a wonderful amber colour. The nose is powerful and demonstrates characteristic *rancio* and woody notes, with honey-like nuances. A pleasant, long-lasting perfume shows on the finish.

Family Reserve

The rarest of the Hine Cognacs is made from good years of Grande Champagne cognacs kept in the family's private cellar. Coloured a rich, deep amber, it shows an unmistakable strength of character on the nose. The elegant bouquet is richly aromatic, mingling many perfumes: among them vanilla, mushrooms and wildflowers. The palate is full-flavoured, so full that it lingers long after the first or second sip has been swallowed.

P240: THESE EMPTY GLASSES PROMISE A TREAT FOR A PROFESSIONAL TASTER OR SOMEONE WITH SUCH A PASSION FOR COGNAC AS MYSELF!

JEAN FILLIOUX

Founded by Honoré Fillioux in 1880 in the heart of Grande Champagne country – at the property La Pouyade in Juillac-Le-Coq – the company is currently run by his great-grandson, Pascal Fillioux, who prudently handles the treasures in the family's *chai* and travels the world explaining the secrets of their success. He and his team control every aspect of their exclusively Grande Champagne *premier cru* cognac's life. Its personality? Floral, fruity, rich, complex, powerful and long on the palate.

La Pouyade
8 years old
A Grande Champagne with an amber colour and ripe greengage and apricot flavours, with a hint of almond and fine vanilla on the palate. A lingering finish rounds it off.

Star 2000
A 17-year-old Grande Champagne cognac with a bright, golden-amber colour. It is fine and fresh on the nose, with dried apricot and jammy mandarine aromas, followed by floral hints of spring flowers and jasmine. Mellow and fat on the palate, it offers rose-petal flavours with hints of cocoa and quince. Incredibly long on the finish, too.

Très Vieux and XO Impérial
23 to 25 years old
This is an amber cognac, with an appetizing aroma of orange marmalade, pears, quince, bananas, citrus, sandalwood and port. On the palate, there are overtones of tropical fruits (maracuja and mango). Long, lingering and very pleasant.

LEOPOLD GOURMEL

This house was founded in 1979 by Pierre Voisin, who is fascinated by the changes in a cognac as it ages: the transformation from young, fruity flavours to floral notes in middle age and then to spice in later life. Each cognac made here is from a single growth and a single vintage from both Fins Bois and Petite Champagne vineyards.

Léopold Gourmel was named Cognac of the Year by both *The Wine Enthusiast* and *Food & Wine Magazine*.

Quintessence
30 years old
This cognac is medium-amber in colour. The aroma has a dominant fruity note with a wisp of smoke. The palate is well-balanced and dry, showing a hint of spice, along with a distinct note of pear and apple. The finish is crisp and dry.

Age des Fleurs
12 to 13 years old
This cognac boasts a fine gold colour with sweet, grassy aromas and hints of apricot dominant on the nose. The body is big, and the dry palate shows notes of violets, cinnamon, nutmeg and oak. The finish is long, crisp and dry.

LHERAUD

A family concern dating back to 1680 when Alexandre Lhéraud cultivated a vineyard in Lasdoux, in the heart of Petite Champagne in the Charente region. In 1795, his son, Augustin Lhéraud, grew grapes on a 25-hectare site; in 1875, Eugène Lhéraud bought an alambic copper still. By 1931, Rémy Lhéraud had become a wine-grower and distiller. In 1970, Guy Lhéraud inherited the land from his father, Rémy. Today, the vineyards cover 125 acres, planted 10 per cent Colombard and 10 per cent Folle Blanche; the rest are Ugni Blanc. This combination gives the cognacs a full-bodied, dry character. The firm also offers vintage cognacs dating from 1965 to 1980, approved by the BNIC.

Cuvée 10
A Petite Champagne cognac aged for 10 years in oak, with a soft, golden colour. On the nose, it is fiery, with aromas of flowers and summer fruits. On the palate, it offers a light vanilla flavour, and a short but delicate finish.

Cuvée 20
Aged more than 20 years
A warm, amber-coloured spirit, with an outstanding aroma of flowers. Smooth on the palate, with a long finish.

LOUIS ROYER

Since 1853, the house of Louis Royer has specialized in buying *eaux-de-vie* from distilleries in five of the six *crus*. This philosophy has been followed by the family over the centuries. Royer is the first house to present a single *cru* distilled at a single distillery. In the Distilleries Collection, the specific flavour of each region is represented, so that cognac-lovers will learn to discern the difference between a Bons Bois distilled at one distillery in that region, and a Grande Champagne distilled at one in its region.

Distillerie Des Saules
8 years old
A Borderie cognac, light amber in colour, with aromas of liquorice and flowers on the nose. The palate is full-bodied with a long structure topped off by a round and dulcet finish.

Distillerie de l'Ecole
12 years old
A Petite Champagne cognac; amber with reddish highlights. On the nose, floral aromas (lime blossom) appear, before evolving into crystallized fruit. The palate is rich, with sustained length and a great mellowness. A long finish allows for maximum enjoyment.

Distillerie les Magnolias
15 years old
This Grande Champagne cognac has a deep, amber colour. On the nose, floral aromas rub shoulders with a hint of crystallized fruit (apricots and prunes) and well-integrated oak. On the palate, a remarkable mellowness leads to a long finish.

ABOVE: DELAMAIN ADOPTED THE POWERFUL EAGLE AS A TRADEMARK FOR ITS EGYPTIAN ADVERTISING.

MARTELL

Founded in 1715 by Jean Martell, from the Channel island of Jersey, a man who married well twice. Aggressive in the international market, Martell has been heading in a new direction, bringing out new cognacs aimed at younger drinkers. Here are my favourites from the company's older collections.

VSOP Médaillon
Created in 1874, Martell VSOP Médaillon bears the image of Louis XIV to celebrate 1715, the last year of the 'Sun King's' reign and the first of Martell's. In colour, it is golden amber. Light, grapey aromas appear on the nose, together with some wood and a touch of vanilla. Finesse and character shine on the palate, which is smooth and mellow, with some complexity. Dry, yet fruity and full, with a hint of sweetness, and good length.

Cordon Bleu
Since its creation by Edouard Martell in 1912, Cordon Bleu has become a legend in its own right. Some 200 *eaux-de-vie* are married in this blend, which introduces itself with a deep, golden-copper colour. On the nose, it is round and complex, floral and spicy. On the palate, it is exceptionally smooth and round, rich in fruit and wood, with a delicate aftertaste due to long ageing. Mellow and complex on the finish.

L'Or de J & F Martell
Launched in 1992 and blended from *eaux-de-vie* from the *paradis*, this copper-coloured cognac is intense, powerful and complex on the nose. On the palate, it is dense with rich, concentrated flavours including a hint of hazelnut. Generous stuff, with an intense finish.

J P MENARD & FILS

The family distillery has been located in Saint-Même-les-Carrières since 1815. In 1946, Jean-Paul Ménard registered the name of the current business, J P Ménard & Fils. His three sons now own 80 hectares in the Grande Champagne region; cognac stocks equal more than half a million bottles, and are divided among several ageing cellars on the family estates. Currently, five qualities of different ages are bottled for sale. They are fortunate to have a *paradis* filled with jewels of ancient cognac, one bottle dating back to before the French Revolution of 1789 and hundreds dated 1818 and 1830.

XO
20 to 25 years old
This cognac shows a lovely amber colour with golden reflections. The nose offers a great aromatic variety of spices and fresh floral notes. On the palate, vanilla, tobacco and cocoa flavours mix harmoniously. *Rancio* notes mark the finish.

Ancestrale
A powerful cognac, lovely amber in colour, with strong scents on the nose due to its 45° of alcohol. On the palate, intense *rancio* tones ride on a palate that is exceptionally long in the mouth.

MENUET

A small producer based in Saint-Même-les-Carrières, along the road from Croizet Cognacs, on the east side of the Grande Champagne region just outside Jarnac. This house is run by David Croizet, who is no relation to the Croizet cognac family.

Menuet owns 50 hectares, where vines are planted. The house was founded in 1850, and in 1900 it won a gold medal at the Paris World Fair. Today, the family concentrates on the high end of the market, selling mainly to private French customers.

Menuet XO
A Grande Champagne cognac with deep-amber to copper hues. The aroma is mushroomy and earthy. On the palate, it is lean and dry, with more earthy flavours. A good, lengthy finish ends the dance.

Menuet Grande Champagne
50 years old
A very deep gold to rich-brown colour, with aromas of butterscotch, toffee, vanilla, fruit cake and Madeira. On the palate, rich toffee, walnut and fruit-cake flavours mingle with *rancio* notes. Long, with waves of flavours.

A C MEUKOW & CO

Formed by two brothers, August and Karl Meukow, and Cognaçais Charles Levoire in 1862, Meukow is now owned by the Compagnie de Guyenne. It produces top-quality cognacs and is a supplier to the House of Lords in London, and the White House in Washington, DC.

VSOP Superior
The percentage of older Cognacs is higher than in a regular VSOP, its average age being 12 years old. An unusual combination of Grande Champagne and older Fins Bois Cognacs. Well-balanced and winey on the palate, with hints of bananas, cinnamon, vanilla and coffee, and a strong finish.

Napoléon
15 years old
This cognac is made of Fins Bois, Petite and Grande Champagne cognacs. The result is an exercise in smoothness, coloured an intense, deep, luminous red. It has the delicacy of dried plums on the nose and palate, with a hint of spice, all rolling towards a long finish.

XO
At 20 to 25 years old, and made with Grande and Petite Champagne cognacs, this is coloured a deep amber, with hints of dry fruit and vanilla on the nose, and a lingering spicy aftertaste.

OTARD

In 1795, Baron Jean-Baptiste Antoine Otard founded this company in the Château du Cognac, birthplace of François I, adjacent the River Charente in the centre of Cognac. Incidentally, the thick walls create unique ageing conditions. Blended from the four finest *crus*, Otard distils on the lees to capture different aromas.

The company buys from distillers in the Grande and Petite Champagne regions, and also in the Borderies. Two other houses, Gaston de la Grange and Exshaw, are under the same slate roof.

VSOP
8 years old
A blend of Fine Champagne cognacs; amber in colour. Aromas of vanilla and spices and a floral hint. The palate is dry, with floral flavours. The finish is long and pleasant.

XO
A blend of very old Grande and Petite Champagne cognac, and a touch of Borderies, with an average age of 35 years. Rich and golden, this sports leather, spices and dried fruits on the nose, and on the palate the flavours are delicate and balanced – and long.

PRINCE HUBERT DE POLIGNAC

The prestige brand of a cooperative in Cognac called Unicoop, the company was founded in 1931 and is made up of some 3,700 vintners. In the late 1980s, the cognac house of Henri Mounier joined the cooperative, which sells to the Court of Her Majesty the Queen of Denmark.

VSOP
5 to 7 years old
Grande and Petite Champagne with Fins Bois cognac. This boasts a mature, amber colour. On the nose it is delicate, with scents of vine flowers and prunes. The palate is full-bodied, with vanilla touches. Subtly flavoured, with a long finish, this is more intense in the mouth than on the nose.

XO
20 to 25 years old
Deep amber in colour, and fully enriched with oaky tannins, this cognac smells of damp old cellars on the nose, before evolving complex aromas of undergrowth and candied fruits alongside floral hints of lilac. On the palate, a sweet, overwhelming and muffled first impression is followed by an aromatic persistence of flavour, called the 'peacock-tail effect' by connoisseurs. Refined right down to the finish.

Premier Grande Cru Grande Champagne
Exclusively a blend of Grande Champagne cognacs, this spirit has a warm, amber colour, enhanced by flashes of mahogany. On the nose, there is an explosion of floral and fruity aromas, ranging from irises to candied fruits. The palate shows a light intensity, delicate harmony and lingering flavours of incense or tropical woods such as cedar – surprising! A soft finish adds just the right touch.

OPPOSITE: THE MAITRE DE CHAI'S DESK WHERE HE SAMPLES THE COGNACS AT VARIOUS STAGES.

350

RAYMOND RAGNAUD

Since 1850, several generations of the family have cultivated 47 hectares of vineyards planted with Ugni Blanc and Folle Blanche grapes in the Grande Champagne region. The two heirs of Raymond Ragnaud – Jean-Marie Ragnaud and Madame Françoise Ragnaud-Bricq – run the business, with the blends created by *maître de chai* Françoise from *eaux-de-vie* distilled in two Charentais pot stills on the property.

Réserve Rare
18 years old
Amber colour with a fresh nose. Vigorous and mellow on the palate, revealing the flavour and richness of port mixed with old wood. A pleasant structure merges into an elegant finish.

Extra Vieux OU XO
25 years old
Amber-coloured, powerful and refined cognac; 42 per cent abv. On the nose, a fruity intensity brings elegance to mind, which is enhanced by a long-lasting finish.

Très Vieille Grande Champagne
50 years old
An exceptional marriage of *eaux-de-vie* of the same year. Coloured a deep amber, it has a vigorous and powerful nose. On the palate, it is rich and persistent, with wood, tobacco, and nuttiness. A fragrant finish rounds it off.

REMY MARTIN

Founded in 1724, by wine-grower Rémy Martin and his brothers, the company has a heritage of quality with its exclusively Fine Champagne cognacs.

The present firm was formed in 1925, under the auspices of André Renaud, a visionary who pursued the concept of producing only Fine Champagne cognacs. When he died in 1965, he left the company to his two daughters and a son-in-law, André Hériard-Dubreuil, who took control and was instrumental in putting together the alliance that created the Rémy-Cointreau Group. Currently, the cognac house is now under the presidency of his daughter, Dominique Hériard-Dubreuil.

1738 Accord Royal
Rich copper-amber in colour, with aromas of oak, cinnamon, ginger and cloves, ending in fine, fruity notes (candied oranges and prunes). There are also hints of honey, vanilla, chocolate, chestnuts and toasted bread. On the palate, mellowness dominates notes of oak. Intense yet delicate.

Extra
A blend of Grande and Petite Champagne of up to 50 years old, Extra was created as a companion to a cigar. Dark amber with yellow tones, it offers the scent of jasmine and delicate aromas of cigar box, walnuts, dried and candied fruits. On the palate, notes of walnuts, saffron and nutmeg give it an exceptional finish.

Louis XIII
A limited edition of 10,000 bottles a year are produced. Aged more than 50 years, this dark, amber-gold spirit boasts aromas of exotic fruits, nuts, cocoa, and tobacco, with a floral background. It is lively on the long palate, with a hint of spice, followed by honey.

ROULLET

Since 1780, the Roullet family has been established in Foussignac on the banks of the River Charente. In 1791, Paul-Frédéric received a new distiller's licence, was acknowledged by the new Republic and became a supplier to the armies of Napoléon. In 1783, Roullet began to sell its cognacs in Paris. For a short time the family was associated with their cousins, the Delamains.

In 1950, Serge Roullet took over and was joined by Mathias Paul Roullet, the eighth-generation family member to guide the company. The estate produces single-vintage, single-vineyard cognacs for the world market. XO is the only blend.

Roullet Vieille Réserve
A single-estate cognac bottled around its 15th year. The nose is firm and dry, with fruity aromas. The palate is rich, round, gingery and dry, with delicate fruit and a spicy touch from the oak. A spirity nip marks the finish.

XO Gold
Awarded a silver medal at the 1996 International Spirits Challenge, this is a blend of cognacs matured for up to 35 years, presented in a gold-topped decanter. Deep amber in colour, it shows delicate aromas of lilac and figs. The palate is smooth and rounded, with a long, delicate finish.

TIFFON

Founded in 1875 by Médéric Tiffon, this family-owned company owns 40 hectares of vineyards in the Grande Champagne and Fins Bois regions, using Ugni Blanc grapes. Tiffon buys wine from over 350 growers for its two distilleries, running 17 Charentais pot stills. The stock level is 15,000 oak casks, which are kept in cellars in Triac, Barbezieux, Fosniac and Jarnac. A recent family disagreement saw Philippe Brastaad-Tiffon leave the company and set up his own cognac house (*see* page 232).

VSOP Fine Champagne Cognac
Aged for between 10 to 15 years in oak, the aroma is rich. It is fruity on the palate, with a hint of vanilla. The long finish is filled with lingering fruit flavours.

XO Fine Champagne
In this blend, the minimum age is 12 and the maximum is 25 years old. This is a fine, gold-coloured spirit, with an aroma of grapes, flowers, a touch of lime blossom and violet. The palate reveals spicy vanilla tones, along with dense, musky flavours which end in a strong finish.

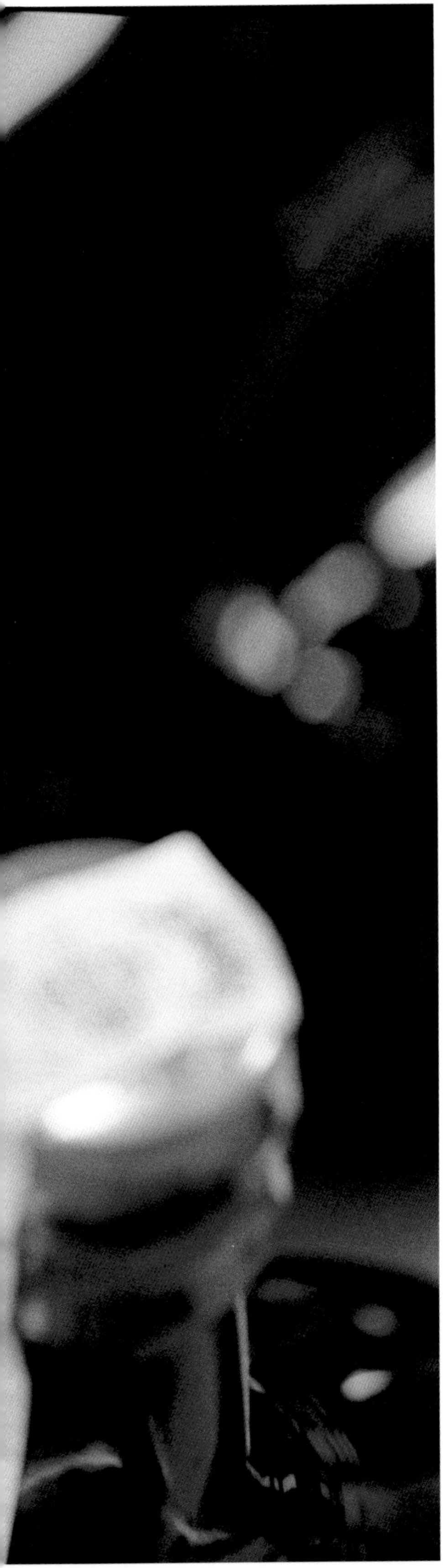

TIPS OF THE TRADE

'I like the treasure chest thrill of opening a cigar box and the accompanying cognac aromas.'

BEATRICE COINTREAU

WHEN IT COMES TO TASTING COGNACS, I AM A TRADITIONALIST, OF THAT THERE CAN BE NO DOUBT. This section deals with tasting cognacs of a decent age, by which I mean starting with a VSOP over 10 years old. I would like to introduce you to cognac the way *I* know it, and in that way I hope to enable you to gain even more pleasure from your next sip of this noble spirit.

P252: SEALED AND READY FOR THE CORK TO BE POPPED; ANOTHER EXQUISITE EXPERIENCE AWAITS A COGNAC LOVER.

An important point made to me by the house of Delamain concerns quality and age. The hierarchy of cognacs (VS, VSOP, Napoléon, XO, etc) is determined by official age and price; this, however, does not necessarily determine quality. There are excellent cognacs of modest rank; there are also disappointing expensive Fine Champagne examples on the market.

In my opinion, an old cognac should be chosen appropriate to the occasion. A Grande Champagne, for instance, requires a relaxed, unhurried attitude in order to appreciate it fully; grabbing a 'window' in the early evening is simply not good enough. Without the right approach, a cognac's true character will remain undiscovered and unappreciated – and you, as a connoisseur, will be deprived of an extraordinary experience. Without further ado, then let us examine some tips of the trade which will allow you to make the most of tasting good cognac.

THE GLASS

Let us begin with the glass. For tasting, I always use a fine glass, preferably in the shape of a newly opened tulip. This shape of glass allows the different aromas to rise gently and gradually, enabling you to savour them; in contrast, the balloon glass, so beloved of vintage movies, concentrates the aromas and releases them too suddenly.

Rinse the glass with plain hot water – detergents leave a residual film that can affect the taste of the spirit. Drain the water well, and avoid wiping the inside of the glass.

The best way to prepare a glass for tasting is to pour in a drop of cognac, swirl it around and then throw it away. This may seem extravagant, but it is important. To serve, pour between three to four centilitres into a standard tulip glass. It's better to have a second nip than to pour a double amount, which will be too strong for the size of the glass. Holding the glass in the palm of the hand provides all the warming that is required. Do not attempt to hold the glass over a flame – ever. This is a terrible error of judgement and a social *faux pas*.

THE ELEMENTS OF TASTING

I agree with Bernard Hine when he says that tasting is something you do with all five senses. 'You taste with your eyes, nose, mouth and hand,' he explains. 'Feeling the glass is important, and if you are clever, you can also taste with your ears as you clink your glass with a friend to wish each other good health.'

There is a common accepted perception that 80 per cent of the appreciation of cognac is taken in via the nose. In my opinion, however, the perfect harmony of nose and the palate is necessary, because it is the palate that distinguishes the cognac's strength, age and character.

According to Olivier Paultes at Frapin, with whom I have tasted a few exceptional old cognacs, there are three stages of appreciating a Grande Champagne cognac. The first two are carried out by professional tasters before the cognac is reduced to 40 per cent alcohol by the addition of distilled water.

Firstly, a taster notes the cognac's appearance, then positions his or her nose a few centimetres away from the rim of the glass. After five years in oak, the cognac will be more brilliant yellow than amber. It will be sweet and mellow, all the flavours will be better combined, floral hints will be present, and fruit will make an appearance, usually reminiscent of apricot jam.

After 10 years, the colour will have progressed from bright-yellow to a more mature and soft golden-yellow. The aromas will be well-balanced and harmonious. Wooden aromas merge with vanilla; hints of port-like characters appear, and an aroma of dried flowers will be present.

OPPOSITE: READY FOR THE BLENDER: A METAL LID KEEPS THE AROMAS IN THE GLASS UNTIL HE WHISKS OFF THE LID AND APPLIES HIS 'NOSE' TO THE LIQUID.

After 15 years, the cognac turns a light, golden brown. Its aromas and flavour are rich and full; the port and wooden vanilla aromas are intense. There is a softness and a balance to the composition, with dried-flower tones more apparent, with spices such as pepper, cinnamon and cloves.

After 20 years, the cognac is brown, the woody aroma has departed, and the floral fragrances are at their best – especially jasmine. A hint of port is still to be found, as is a hint of woody vanilla. Cognacs of 30 years and over are much more floral and complex.

The second stage is made once the cognac has been swirled in the glass, and the nose moved closer to the rim. With a five-year-old, you will notice a complex combination of fruity and floral aromas (lime and rose); with a

10-year-old, the port element is more persistent, and there is a touch of spice (cinnamon and pepper) as well as curry. A 15-year-old will have an aroma of dried fruit, grilled almonds, and walnuts. After 20 years, the floral aroma will have developed, along with spicy, dried fruits – particularly apricots – and nuts.

The third stage of tasting involves the act of tasting. A five-year-old spirit includes long-lasting woody vanilla, rose petals and fruity apricot aromas and flavours. A 10-year-old has a delicate hint of port and more perceptible spicy-curry tones and the bouquet is intense and full.

After 15 years, the spicy character disappears; there is a heady sense of dried roses as well as a hint of jasmine and tobacco. After 20 years, even headier characteristics develop, as does the aroma of dried fruit, and the cognac will be very floral. In addition, an entirely new set of flavours and aromas appear, known as *rancio*, characterized by crushed nuts, leather, chocolate, almonds and preserved orange peel, followed by soft, spicy elements.

The Delamains are also lyrical about the unfolding of aromas. 'When a great cognac develops its aromatic complexity in the glass,' they write in their notes on tasting, 'one can truly say it is playing an olfactory score. It would be a shame to miss this performance by drinking the cognac too fast.'

Thus, a Petite Champagne cognac will reveal more fruity, floral aromas; the Borderies' spirits have hints of irises and violets typical of the region; and Fins Bois cognacs are typically reminiscent of ripe fruit.

I recommend taking tiny sips to tease and delight the senses, letting the cognac fan out on the palate by keeping your mouth closed and 'chewing' it for a moment or two. Surprises even arise when you leave a glass nearly empty. For example, one night when I was tasting a newly acquired pre-phylloxera cognac and making notes for my files, I left the almost-empty glass in front of me. I had poured only a tiny amount to taste: the first intense aromas were purely floral and woody, with a hint of spice. Then, after about half an hour, I checked the residue in the glass again: it had become mustier with a hint of vanilla, and later still, it became softer and softer, with cocoa dominant.

In an old cognac especially, the fragrance is so powerful that it stays with you in your throat, then starts to develop on your palate. If it is less complex, the taste will stay for a shorter time, and you will need to go back to the glass to revive that experience.

Above all, it is important to develop a taste memory of aromas and flavours, then choose which most closely matches anything stored in this memory-bank. That way, you will learn to distinguish one aroma from another.

COGNAC AND CIGARS

Not surprisingly, cigar *aficionados* look for different aspects in a cognac. Since the flavour of a cigar is strong, the cognac needs aromas and flavours that complement it. Béatrice Cointreau, chief executive and managing director of Frapin, is an ardent cigar-smoker, having been enthralled by the smoke from her father's cigar at an early age. What follows is her advice on matching a quality cigar with a quality cognac.

A VSOP with its honey and spicy characteristics and dried-fruit aromas is good with lighter cigars and Panatelas. An XO quality with *rancio* (nuts and dried fruits mixed with dried flowers and a complex bouquet) and long-lasting aromas is perfect for Coronas, Cedros de Luxe and Exhibition No 4. An older, mature cognac is recommended for the best Montecristos, Romeo and Juliettas,

Fabulosos and Espledidos: something with a lingering finish in which all the flavours of a complex cognac meld harmoniously with the aromas of the cigar.

STORING COGNAC IN A BOTTLE

The edict here is to stand the bottle upright. If it is lies on its side. the cork can have an unpleasant reaction with the cognac. Consider the room or cellar temperature: most prefer being stored at a reasonable room temperature and away from light. Older cognacs, particularly Grande Champagnes, are sensitive to cold, and may acquire a cloudy look. This is not a failure. This reaction to cold is proof that they still have all of the elements which give the brandy its bouquet, flavour and roundness. I recommend that you do not leave a bottle uncorked for longer than the time required to fill a glass. Once opened, cognac has a limited life – perhaps six to eight months – before its characteristics will change. Try to finish the bottle within that period.

OPPOSITE: THE HYDROMETRE IS AN EVERYDAY TOOL USED TO ASCERTAIN THE ALCOHOLIC POTENTIAL OF THE SPIRIT.

OPENING A BOTTLE

If a bottle has heavy wax covering the cap, do not chip at the wax too aggressively, as you may break off part of the neck. Instead, run the cap under a hot tap to soften the wax, then make an incision in the wax which will let you work the point of the knife in under it and prize it away. If you have a bottle of rare vintage cognac botle in which the cork has shrunk and you need to replace it, take it to a reputable cognac dealer (or an auction house such as Sotheby's, Bonham's or Christie's), who will recommend the appropriate action to take. This is not something to try yourself at home.

Delamain & C°
COGNAC
Delamain & C°
COGNAC
Delamain & C°
COGNAC

Delamain & Cie
COGNAC
le 11. Mai. 99
402
Cognac
cpte 8
Delamain
COGNAC
Delamain & Cie
COGNAC
Delamain & Cie
COGNAC

GLOSSARY

Acquit	Document required by every load of spirit carried on a public road.
Appellation d'Origine Controlée	Legal term that guarantees a cognac's geographical origin, method of production and the grapes from which is has been produced. It is awarded only when the product conforms with the regulations.
Bonne chauffe	Second distillation of *eau-de-vie* that produces cognac.
Brandewijn	Old Dutch word for 'burnt wine', which the English adopted as 'brandy' in the 17th century (also *brandvin, brandywijn*).
Brouillis	The half-strength, colourless spirit produced after the first distillation.
Chai	A warehouse used for storing cognac in cask.
Chapiteau	French word for the 'big top': the small, round container that traps the alcoholic vapours that drift up from the alembic positioned below.
Chauffe	French word for the heating process in cognac production, used for a single pass through the still; there are two: *la première* and *la bonne*.
Col de cygne	The modern, 'swan-neck-shaped' neck of the still.
Colombard	Grape variety planted to produce sweet wines, also used to produce a particularly fragrant cognac.
Comptes	Term describing the age of cognacs.
Cru	Literally 'growth', figuratively a vineyard or region. The French term used to indicate the six regions of the Cognac *appellation*.
Early Landed cognacs	Term used to describe cognacs shipped when they are young, in cask, to a British warehouse, usually in Bristol.
Eau-de-vie	'Water of life'. Distilled spirit, usually from fruit.
Gabelle	Salt tax levied from the Middle Ages until the 1780s (*see* p38).

P262/3: SAMPLES ARE INTEGRAL TO THE HISTORY OF EVERY COGNAC THAT IS DEVELOPED AND BLENDED.

Lees	(French: *Lie*) The sediment composed mainly of dead yeast cells left in a wine vat after fermentation.
Limousin	Type of wood used for one of the two types of French casks.
Maître de chai	The cellar-master, is responsible for looking after the cognac in cask, the blending, and dilution of the cognac.
Napoléon	Term applied to a specific quality of cognac that is above VSOP and below XO.
Paradis	A special cellar used for storing old cognacs.
Queues	The 'tails': the last part of a run of cognac through the still.
Rancio	A rich, burnt or nutty flavour developed by some wines as they age in wood; used to describe the flavour of certain cognacs.
Serpentin	The cooling coil attached to the still.
Terroir	Term used to describe a combination of soil, climate, geographical position, etc, of a vineyard that affect the taste of wine produced from it.
Tête	The 'head' of the cognac: first trickle of spirit to emerge from distillation.
Tonnelier	Cooper or cask-maker.
Tronçais	One of two types of oak used to make casks, from north of Cognac.
Ugni Blanc	Main grape variety used in the production of post-phylloxera cognac.

DEFINITIONS OF COGNAC TYPES

Cognac: a spirit distilled from wine in the Charente region of western France.

Fine Cognac: a brandy of no great distinction.

Eau-de-vie des Charente: another term for cognac.

Grande Champagne or Grande Fine Champagne: 100 per cent Grande Champagne cognac.

Petite Champagne or Petite Fine Champagne: 100 per cent Petite Champagne cognac.

Fine Champagne: the finest cognac, blended exclusively from Grande and Petite Champagne cognac, with a minimum of 50 per cent of Grande Champagne cognac.

Borderies or Fines Borderies: 100 per cent Borderies cognac.

Fins Bois or Fine Fins Bois: 100 per cent Fins Bois cognac.

Bons Bois or Fine Bons Bois: 100 per cent Bons Bois cognac.

La Chaise
Veillard
RESERVE
DE
CHASSE

Note: the term *Fine* is authorized by a 1938 law to designate a cognac from a controlled appellation. For example, a Grande Fine Champagne is a controlled appellation Grande Champagne cognac containing 100 per cent cognac from the Grande Champagne district. The Fine Champagne controlled appellation is given to a cognac that is a blend exclusively of Grande and Petite Champagne Cognacs, with a minimum 50 per cent of Grande Champagne. These terms are now categorized by the BNIC regulations.

QUALITIES OF COGNACS

*****Three Star/VS:** the youngest cognac is three years old.
VSOP or VO Very Special (or Superior) Old Pale: the youngest cognac is between five and six years old.
Napoléon, Grande Réserve and Extra Vieille: the youngest cognac is at least six years old.
XO: the youngest cognac is usually at least 15 years old.

Generally speaking, houses use cognacs that are older than the minimum requirement. Those used in the prestigious labels may have been matured for between 20 to 40 years.

APPENDIX

There are six *comptes*, or index figures, in the code that controls the labelling and sale of cognac:

0 = brandy as being of the year of distillation
1 = more than one year old
2 = more than two years old
3 = more than three years old
4 = more than four years old
5 = more than five years old

The main market for cognac in 1999 was the United States, with 35.8 million bottles; the majority being VS, superior qualities in the minority. These figures are up 4.25 per cent on the previous year.

The United Kingdom was second, with 11.1 million bottles, with the same ratio of VS to superior qualities. This market was down 0.7 per cent on the previous year.

The local French market was up 14.5 per cent at 9.2 million bottles; Japan was down 32.1 per cent with 6.9 million bottles. Hong Kong took 5 million bottles of superior-quality cognac only,

P266/7: LATE WINTER – THE VINES SLEEP AS ANOTHER DAY CLOSES IN THE ENCHANTING COGNAC REGION.
P272: A CLOSED HEAVY TIMBER DOOR IS LIKELY TO BE GAURDING SOME OF COGNAC'S RICH HISTORY.

and Singapore took 4.1 million of superior-quality only. With exports representing 91.8 per cent of total production, cognac accounts for about two-thirds of a month's worth of France's annual trade surplus (approximately 7.7 billion francs). In terms of hectolitres of pure alcohol, 376,429 left Cognac's cellars in 1999. That is the equivalent of 134.4 million bottles.

There was an overall increase of 2.3 per cent in sales to the European Union, an encouraging sign for the future. Exports to Norway increased by a remarkable 38 per cent: the figures are 8,340 hectolitres of pure alcohol compared to just 6,030 hectolitres the previous year.

The European market had to face the abolition of duty-free sales on July 1, 1999, and figures reflect a 12.4 per cent decrease in sales. Asia's economic situation remains fragile, yet it is improving slightly quicker than forecast. Japan remains an uncertain market, with a tightening of the economic belt still very much in evidence.

ACKNOWLEDGMENTS

I would like to thank all of the people that I have met on my memorable journey to here, the end of this book. It is simply not possible to write a book on cognac without the cooperation of many people and sipping quite a bit of this silken amber liquid.

Thanks to writer Lynn Bryan, who worked with me to capture the spirit of cognac in words, and I would like to thank all of those people who shared with us both their unlimited knowledge and genuine hospitality during our visits to Cognac, including Maurice Hennessy, Bernard Hine, Jacques Rivière, Jean-Paul Camus, the team at Courvoisier, Max Cointreau, Béatrice Cointreau and Olivier Paultes at Frapin, Georges Clot and Tim Banks at Rémy Martin, Mary J Rullier at Croizet, Judith Menier at Martell, the Musée du Cognac, Seguin Moreau, Charles Braastad-Delamain and Philippe Braastad-Tiffon.

At The Bureau Interprofessional du Cognac, thanks to its Communications Director Claire Coates, and also to Dominique Lherahoux-Cornette.

I would also like to thank Jason Lowe, the photographer, for his magnificent contribution to this celebration of cognac. And, as ever, thanks to my agent, Fiona Lindsay, and to Cassell & Co for believing in my dream of liquid history.

PICTURE CREDITS

All photography is by Jason Lowe unless stated otherwise. The publishers are grateful to the following: p13 map artwork by Kenny Grant; p19 Hennessy; p21 Courvoisier; p27 Hennessy; p31 Martell; p45 Bridgeman Art Gallery; p59 Martell; p63 Martell; p71 Rémy Martin; p107 Hine; p125 Rémy Martin; p133 Martell; p173 Martell; p191 Hennessy; pp230/1 Musée de la Ville de Cognac.

INDEX